Whether you are walking the path of spiritual growth, seeking guidance or comfort, telling someone or a group about God's Word, or merely wanting to quote a timely passage from the Bible, this collection will provide the right Scripture for every need.

This topical reference book is meant to encourage in-depth study of the Bible and a deeper hunger for the Word of God.

Each Scripture selection should be read in context in the Bible whenever possible and should be used with other available source material.

May the Lord richly bless you as He speaks to you through His Living Word!

DISTRIBUTED BY
Choice Books
Salunga, PA 17538
We Welcome Your Response

My Book
of
Bible
Promises

The Right Scripture
For Every Need

A BARBOUR BOOK

Leatherette Edition ISBN 1-55748-154-7
Bonded Leather Edition ISBN 1-55748-155-5
Bonded Leather Flexible Edition ISBN 1-55748-156-3

Published by   Barbour and Company, Inc.
               P.O. Box 719
               Uhrichsville, OH 44683

Printed in the United States of America

Contents

Additional Topical References ..274

Where to Find It In the Bible 281

Almighty God....

God's Authority

And God said unto Moses, I AM THAT I AM: and he said, Thus shalt thou say unto the children of Israel, I AM hath sent me unto you.

Exodus 3:14

For thus saith the Lord that created the heavens; God himself that formed the earth and made it; he hath established it, he created it not in vain, he formed it to be inhabited: I am the Lord; and there is none else.

Isaiah 45:18

And when Abram was ninety years old and nine, the Lord appeared to Abram, and said unto him, I am the Almighty God; walk before me, and be thou perfect.

Genesis 17:1

And ye my flock, the flock of my pasture, are men, and I am your God, saith the Lord God.

Ezekiel 34:31

Yet I am the Lord thy God from the land of Egypt, and thou shalt know no god but me: for there is no saviour beside me.

Hosea 13:4

I am the Lord your God; walk in my statutes, and keep my judgments, and do them.

Ezekiel 20:19

God (Creator)

In the beginning God created the heaven and the earth.

Genesis 1:1

For every house is builded by some man; but he that built all things is God.

Hebrews 3:4

Praise ye him, sun and moon: praise him, all ye stars of light. Praise him, ye heavens of heavens, and ye waters that be above the heavens. Let them praise the name of the Lord: for he commanded, and they were created.

Psalm 148:3-5

For by him were all things created, that are in heaven, and that are in earth, visible and invisible, whether they be thrones, or dominions, or principalities, or powers: all things were created by him, and for him.

Colossians 1:16

Through faith we understand that the worlds were framed by the word of God, so that things which are seen were not made of things which do appear.

Hebrews 11:3

By the word of the Lord were the heavens made; and all the host of them by the breath of his mouth.

Psalm 33:6

God Eternal

Lord, thou hast been our dwelling place in all generations. Before the mountains were brought forth, or ever thou hadst formed the earth and the world, even from everlasting to everlasting, thou art God.

Psalm 90:1,2

How great are his signs! and how mighty are his wonders! his kingdom is an everlasting kingdom, and his dominion is from generation to generation.

Daniel 4:3

Now unto the King eternal, immortal, invisible, the only wise God, be honour and glory for ever and ever. Amen.

I Timothy 1:17

The eternal God is thy refuge, and underneath are the everlasting arms.

Deuteronomy 33:27

But thou, O Lord, shalt endure for ever; and thy remembrance unto all generations.

Psalm 102:12

But the Lord is the true God, he is the living God, and an everlasting king.

Jeremiah 10:10

But thou art the same, and thy years shall have no end.

Psalm 102:27

God's Faithfulness

Know therefore that the Lord thy God, he is God, the faithful God, which keepeth covenant and mercy with them that love him and keep his commandments to a thousand generations.

Deuteronomy 7:9

Thy faithfulness is unto all generations: thou hast established the earth, and it abideth.

Psalm 119:90

If we confess our sins, he is faithful and just to forgive us our sins, and to cleanse us from all unrighteousness.

I John 1:9

If we believe not, yet he abideth faithful: he cannot deny himself.

II Timothy 2:13

Wherefore let them that suffer according to the will of God commit the keeping of their souls to him in well doing, as unto a faithful Creator.

I Peter 4:19

Faithful is he that calleth you, who also will do it.

I Thessalonians 5:24

But the Lord is faithful, who shall stablish you, and keep you from evil.

II Thessalonians 3:3

God the Father

For ye have not received the spirit of bondage again to fear; but ye have received the Spirit of adoption, whereby we cry, Abba, Father. The Spirit itself beareth witness with our spirit, that we are the children of God.

Romans 8:15,16

After this manner therefore pray ye: Our Father which art in heaven, Hallowed by thy name.

Matthew 6:9

...O foolish people and unwise? is not he thy father that hath bought thee? hath he not made thee, and established thee?

Deuteronomy 32:6

For ye are all the children of God by faith in Christ Jesus.

Galatians 3:26

If ye then, being evil, know how to give good gifts unto your children, how much more shall your Father which is in heaven give good things to them that ask him?

Matthew 7:11

Have we not all one father? hath not one God created us? ...

Malachi 2:10

God's Favour

But the Lord was with Joseph, and shewed him mercy, and gave him favour in the sight of the keeper of the prison.

Genesis 39:21

And I will give this people favour in the sight of the Egyptians: and it shall come to pass, that, when ye go, ye shall not go empty.

Exodus 3:21

For thou, Lord, wilt bless the righteous; with favour wilt thou compass him as with a shield.

Psalm 5:12

Let not mercy and truth forsake thee: bind them about thy neck; write them upon the table of thine heart: So shalt thou find favour and good understanding in the sight of God and man.

Proverbs 3:3,4

A good name is rather to be chosen than great riches, and loving favour rather than silver and gold.

Proverbs 22:1

For they got not the land in possession by their own sword, neither did their own arm save them: but thy right hand, and thine arm, and the light of thy countenance, because thou hadst a favour unto them.

Psalm 44:3

God's Glory

Thine, O Lord, is the greatness, and the power, and the glory, and the victory, and the majesty: for all that is in the heaven and in the earth is thine; thine is the kingdom, O Lord, and thou art exalted as head above all.

I Chronicles 29:11

And the city had no need of the sun, neither of the moon, to shine in it: for the glory of God did lighten it, and the Lamb is the light thereof.

Revelation 21:23

And the glory of the Lord shall be revealed, and all flesh shall see it together: for the mouth of the Lord hath spoken it.

Isaiah 40:5

And, lo, the angel of the Lord came upon them, and the glory of the Lord shone round about them: and they were sore afraid.

Luke 2:9

And the sight of the glory of the Lord was like devouring fire on the top of the mount in the eyes of the children of Israel.

Exodus 24:17

And when I could not see for the glory of that light.

Acts 22:11

God's Goodness

Every good gift and every perfect gift is from above, and cometh down from the Father of lights, with whom is no variableness, neither shadow of turning.

James 1:17

Oh how great is thy goodness, which thou hast laid up for them that fear thee; which thou hast wrought for them that trust in thee before the sons of men!

Psalm 31:19

Oh that men would praise the Lord for his goodness, and for his wonderful works to the children of men!

Psalm 107:8

Or despisest thou the riches of his goodness and forbearance and longsuffering; not knowing that the goodness of God leadeth thee to repentance?

Romans 2:4

He loveth righteousness and judgment: the earth is full of the goodness of the Lord.

Psalm 33:5

Nevertheless he left not himself without witness, in that he did good, and gave us rain from heaven, and fruitful seasons, filling our hearts with food and gladness.

Acts 14:17

God's Graciousness

And the Lord passed by before him, and proclaimed, The Lord, The Lord God, merciful and gracious, longsuffering, and abundant in goodness and truth.

Exodus 34:6

But the God of all grace, who hath called us unto his eternal glory by Christ Jesus, after that ye have suffered a while, make you perfect, stablish, strengthen, settle you.

I Peter 5:10

Surely he scorneth the scorners: but he giveth grace unto the lowly.

Proverbs 3:34

And the Word was made flesh, and dwelt among us, (and we beheld his glory, the glory as of the only begotten of the Father,) full of grace and truth.

John 1:14

The Lord is merciful and gracious, slow to anger, and plenteous in mercy.

Psalm 103:8

And now, brethren, I commend you to God, and to the word of his grace, which is able to build you up, and to give you an inheritance among all them which are sanctified.

Acts 20:32

Gracious is the Lord, and righteous; yea, our God is merciful.

Psalm 116:5

God's Guidance

Trust in the Lord with all thine heart; and lean not unto thine own understanding. In all thy ways acknowledge him, and he shall direct thy paths.

Proverbs 3:5,6

Now therefore, I pray thee, if I have found grace in thy sight, shew me now thy way, that I may know thee, that I may find grace in thy sight: and consider that this nation is thy people. And he said, My presence shall go with thee, and I will give thee rest.

Exodus 33:13,14

But made his own people to go forth like sheep, and guided them in the wilderness like a flock.

Psalm 78:52

He maketh me to lie down in green pastures: he leadeth me beside the still waters. He restoreth my soul: he leadeth me in the paths of righteousness for his name's sake.

Psalm 23:2,3

I will instruct thee and teach thee in the way which thou shalt go: I will guide thee with mine eye.

Psalm 32:8

For this God is our God for ever and ever: he will be our guide even unto death.

Psalm 48:14

God's Holiness

For I am the Lord that bringeth you up out of the land of Egypt, to be your God: ye shall therefore be holy, for I am holy.

Leviticus 11:45

I am the Lord, your Holy One, the creator of Israel, your King.

Isaiah 43:15

And one cried unto another, and said, Holy, holy, holy, is the Lord of hosts: the whole earth is full of his glory.

Isaiah 6:3

Sing unto the Lord, O ye saints of his, and give thanks at the remembrance of his holiness.

Psalm 30:4

Exalt the Lord our God, and worship at his holy hill; for the Lord our God is holy.

Psalm 99:9

But the Lord of hosts shall be exalted in judgment, and God that is holy shall be sanctified in righteousness.

Isaiah 5:16

So will I make my holy name known in the midst of my people Israel; and I will not let them pollute my holy name any more: and the heathen shall know that I am the Lord, the Holy One in Israel.

Ezekiel 39:7

God's Jealousy

Thou shalt not bow down thyself to them, nor serve them: for I the Lord thy God am a jealous God.

Exodus 20:5

Woe to the rebellious children, saith the Lord, that take counsel, but not of me; and that cover with a covering, but not of my spirit, that they may add sin to sin.

Isaiah 30:1

God is jealous, and the Lord revengeth; the Lord revengeth, and is furious; the Lord will take vengeance on his adversaries, and he reserveth wrath for his enemies.

Nahum 1:2

For the Lord thy God is a consuming fire, even a jealous God.

Deuteronomy 4:24

For thou shalt worship no other god: for the Lord, whose name is Jealous, is a jealous God.

Exodus 34:14

They provoked him to jealousy with strange gods, with abominations provoked they him to anger.

Deuteronomy 32:16

God's Justice

He is the Rock, his work is perfect: for all his ways are judgment: a God of truth and without iniquity, just and right is he.

Deuteronomy 32:4

Yet ye say, The way of the Lord is not equal. Hear now, O house of Israel; Is not my way equal? are not your ways unequal?

Ezekiel 18:25

And if ye call on the Father, who without respect of persons judgeth according to every man's work, pass the time of your sojourning here in fear.

I Peter 1:17

The Lord is slow to anger, and great in power, and will not at all acquit the wicked: the Lord hath his way in the whirlwind and in the storm, and the clouds are the dust of his feet.

Nahum 1:3

Justice and judgment are the habitation of thy throne: mercy and truth shall go before thy face.

Psalm 89:14

Great in counsel, and mighty in work: for thine eyes are open upon all the ways of the sons of men: to give every one according to his ways, and according to the fruit of his doings.

Jeremiah 32:19

God's Love

For God so loved the world, that he gave his only begotten Son, that whosoever believeth in him should not perish, but have everlasting life.

John 3:16

Behold, what manner of love the Father hath bestowed upon us, that we should be called the sons of God.

I John 3:1

And we have known and believed the love that God hath to us. God is love; and he that dwelleth in love dwelleth in God, and God in him.

I John 4:16

For I am persuaded, that neither death, nor life, nor angels, nor principalities, nor powers, nor things present, nor things to come, Nor height, nor depth, nor any other creature, shall be able to separate us from the love of God, which is in Christ Jesus our Lord.

Romans 8:38,39

But God commendeth his love toward us, in that, while we were yet sinners, Christ died for us.

Romans 5:8

God's Lovingkindness

But let him that glorieth glory in this, that he understandeth and knoweth me, that I am the Lord which exercise lovingkindness, judgment, and righteousness, in the earth: for in these things I delight, saith the Lord.

Jeremiah 9:24

Bless the Lord, O my soul, and forget not all his benefits: Who forgiveth all thine iniquities; who healeth all thy diseases; Who redeemeth thy life from destruction; who crowneth thee with lovingkindness and tender mercies.

Psalm 103:2-4

The Lord hath appeared of old unto me, saying, Yea, I have loved thee with an everlasting love: therefore with lovingkindness have I drawn thee.

Jeremiah 31:3

Examine me, O Lord, and prove me; try my reins and my heart. For thy lovingkindness is before mine eyes: and I have walked in thy truth.

Psalm 26:2,3

How excellent is thy lovingkindness, O God! therefore the children of men put their trust under the shadow of thy wings.

Psalm 36:7

God's Majesty

All thy works shall praise thee, O Lord; and thy saints shall bless thee. They shall speak of the glory of thy kingdom, and talk of thy power; To make known to the sons of men his mighty acts, and the glorious majesty of his kingdom.

Psalm 145:10-12

The Lord reigneth, he is clothed with majesty.

Psalm 93:1

Thine, O Lord, is the greatness, and the power, and the glory, and the victory, and the majesty: for all that is in the heaven and in the earth is thine; thine is the kingdom, O Lord, and thou art exalted as head above all.

I Chronicles 29:11

I will speak of the glorious honour of thy majesty, and of thy wondrous works.

Psalm 145:5

The voice of the Lord is powerful; the voice of the Lord is full of majesty.

Psalm 29:4

Now of the things which we have spoken this is the sum: We have such an high priest, who is set on the right hand of the throne of the Majesty in the heavens.

Hebrews 8:1

God's Mercy

And he said, I will make all my goodness pass before thee, and I will proclaim the name of the Lord before thee; and will be gracious to whom I will be gracious, and will shew mercy on whom I will show mercy.

Exodus 33:19

The Lord is gracious, and full of compassion; slow to anger, and of great mercy. The Lord is good to all: and his tender mercies are over all his works.

Psalm 145:8,9

To give knowledge of salvation unto his people by the remission of their sins, Through the tender mercy of our God.

Luke 1:77,78

Who is a God like unto thee, that pardoneth iniquity, and passeth by the transgression of the remnant of his heritage? he retaineth not his anger for ever, because he delighteth in mercy.

Micah 7:18

Yet thou in they manifold mercies forsookest them not in the wilderness.

Nehemiah 9:19

For thou, Lord, art good, and ready to forgive; and plenteous in mercy unto all them that call upon thee.

Psalm 86:5

God's Omnipotence

To whom then will ye liken me, or shall I be equal? saith the Holy One.

Isaiah 40:25

But Jesus beheld them, and said unto them, With men this is impossible; but with God all things are possible.

Matthew 19:26

And in very deed for this cause have I raised thee up, for to shew in thee my power; and that my name may be declared throughout all the earth.

Exodus 9:16

Is any thing too hard for the Lord? . . .

Genesis 18:14

Why should it be thought a thing incredible with you, that God should raise the dead?

Acts 26:8

God hath spoken once; twice have I heard this; that power belongeth unto God.

Psalm 62:11

Trust ye in the Lord for ever: for in the Lord JEHOVAH is everlasting strength.

Isaiah 26:4

God's Omnipresence

Whither shall I go from thy spirit? or whither shall I flee from thy presence? If I ascend up into heaven, thou art there: if I make my bed in hell, behold, thou art there. If I take the wings of the morning, and dwell in the uttermost parts of the sea; Even there shall thy hand lead me, and thy right hand shall hold me.

Psalm 139:7-10

Am I a God at hand, saith the Lord, and not a God afar off? Can any hide himself in secret places that I shall not see him? saith the Lord. Do not I fill heaven and earth? saith the Lord.

Jeremiah 23:23,24

Know therefore this day, and consider it in thine heart, that the Lord he is God in heaven above, and upon the earth beneath: there is none else.

Deuteronomy 4:39

But will God indeed dwell on the earth? behold, the heaven and heaven of heavens cannot contain thee; how much less this house that I have builded?

I Kings 8:27

And he said, My presence shall go with thee, and I will give thee rest.

Exodus 33:14

God's Omniscience

Neither is there any creature that is not manifest in his sight: but all things are naked and opened unto the eyes of him with whom we have to do.

Hebrews 4:13

This then is the message which we have heard of him, and declare unto you, that God is light, and in him is no darkness at all.

I John 1:5

...for your Father knoweth what things ye have need of, before ye ask him.

Matthew 6:8

Talk no more so exceeding proudly; let not arrogancy come out of your mouth: for the Lord is a God of knowledge, and by him actions are weighed.

I Samuel 2:3

For truly my words shall not be false: he that is perfect in knowledge is with thee.

Job 36:4

For the ways of man are before the eyes of the Lord, and he pondereth all his goings.

Proverbs 5:21

He telleth the number of the stars; he calleth them all by their names.

Psalm 147:4

God's Patience

But thou, O Lord, art a God full of compassion, and gracious, longsuffering, and plenteous in mercy and truth.

Psalm 86:15

The Lord is merciful and gracious, slow to anger, and plenteous in mercy. He will not always chide: neither will he keep his anger for ever.

Psalm 103:8,9

And the Lord passed by before him, and proclaimed, The Lord, The Lord God, merciful and gracious, longsuffering, and abundant in goodness and truth.

Exodus 34:6

For my name's sake will I defer mine anger, and for my praise will I refrain for thee, that I cut thee not off.

Isaiah 48:9

And the Lord said, My spirit shall not always strive with man, for that he also is flesh: yet his days shall be an hundred and twenty years.

Genesis 6:3

Nevertheless mine eye spared them from destroying them, neither did I make an end of them in the wilderness.

Ezekiel 20:17

God's Perfection

He is the Rock, his work is perfect: for all his ways are judgment: a God of truth and without iniquity, just and right is he.

Deuteronomy 32:4

As for God, his way is perfect; the word of the Lord is tried: he is a buckler to all them that trust in him.

II Samuel 22:31

The law of the Lord is perfect, converting the soul: the testimony of the Lord is sure, making wise the simple.

Psalm 19:7

Be ye therefore perfect, even as your Father which is in heaven is perfect.

Matthew 5:48

For we know in part, and we prophesy in part. But when that which is perfect is come, then that which is in part shall be done away.

I Corinthians 13:9,10

Dost thou know the balancings of the clouds, the wondrous works of him which is perfect in knowledge?

Job 37:16

God's Protection

Because thou hast made the Lord, which is my refuge, even the most High, thy habitation; There shall no evil befall thee, neither shall any plague come nigh thy dwelling. For he shall give his angels charge over thee, to keep thee in all thy ways. They shall bear thee up in their hands, lest thou dash thy foot against a stone.

Psalm 91:9-12

Ye shall not need to fight in this battle: set yourselves, stand ye still, and see the salvation of the Lord with you, O Judah and Jerusalem: fear not, nor be dismayed; tomorrow go out against them: for the Lord will be with you.

II Chronicles 20:17

Fear thou not; for I am with thee: be not dismayed; for I am thy God: I will strengthen thee; yea, I will help thee; yea, I will uphold thee with the right hand of my righteousness.

Isaiah 41:10

No weapon that is formed against thee shall prosper; and every tongue that shall rise against thee in judgment thou shalt condemn. This is the heritage of the servants of the Lord, and their righteousness is of me, saith the Lord.

Isaiah 54:17

The angel of the Lord encampeth round about them that fear him, and delivereth them.

Psalm 34:7

God's Providence

Thy kingdom is an everlasting kingdom, and thy dominion endureth throughout all generations. The Lord upholdeth all that fall, and raiseth up all those that be bowed down. The eyes of all wait upon thee; and thou givest them their meat in due season. Thou openest thine hand, and satisfiest the desire of every living thing.

Psalm 145:13-16

... and upholding all things by the word of his power.

Hebrews 1:3

For in him we live, and move, and have our being.

Acts 17:28

And we know that all things work together for good to them that love God, to them who are the called according to his purpose.

Romans 8:28

For that ye ought to say, If the Lord will, we shall live, and do this, or that.

James 4:15

... for he maketh his sun to rise on the evil and on the good, and sendeth rain on the just and on the unjust.

Matthew 5:45

God's Righteousness

Hearken unto me, ye that know righteousness, the people in whose heart is my law; fear ye not the reproach of men, neither be ye afraid of their revilings. For the moth shall eat them up like a garment, and the worm shall eat them like wool: but my righteousness shall be for ever, and my salvation from generation to generation.

Isaiah 51:7,8

Fear thou not; for I am with thee: be not dismayed; for I am thy God: I will strengthen thee; yea, I will help thee; yea, I will uphold thee with the right hand of my righteousness.

Isaiah 41:10

O righteous Father, the world hath not known thee: but I have known thee, and these have known that thou hast sent me.

John 17:25

The heavens declare his righteousness, and all the people see his glory.

Psalm 97:6

Thy righteousness is an everlasting righteousness, and thy law is the truth.

Psalm 119:142

Thy righteousness also, O God, is very high, who hast done great things: O God, who is like unto thee!

Psalm 71:19

God's Sovereignty

Thus saith the Lord the King of Israel, and his redeemer the Lord of hosts; I am the first, and I am the last; and beside me there is no God.

Isaiah 44:6

Thou art worthy, O Lord, to receive glory and honour and power: for thou hast created all things, and for thy pleasure they are and were created.

Revelation 4:11

If I were hungry, I would not tell thee: for the world is mine, and the fulness thereof.

Psalm 50:12

That men may know that thou, whose name alone is JEHOVAH, art the most high over all the earth.

Psalm 83:18

Thou shalt have no other gods before me.

Exodus 20:3

For of him, and through him, and to him, are all things: to whom be glory for ever. Amen.

Romans 11:36

...whatsoever is under the whole heaven is mine.

Job 41:11

God's Will

Jesus said unto him, Thou shalt love the Lord thy God with all thy heart, and with all thy soul, and with all thy mind. This is the first and great commandment. And the second is like unto it, Thou shalt love thy neighbour as thyself. On these two commandments hang all the law and the prophets.

Matthew 22:37-40

And this is the will of him that sent me, that every one which seeth the Son, and believeth on him, may have everlasting life: and I will raise him up at the last day.

John 6:40

And be not conformed to this world: but be ye transformed by the renewing of your mind, that ye may prove what is that good, and acceptable, and perfect, will of God.

Romans 12:2

The Lord is not slack concerning his promise, as some men count slackness; but is longsuffering to us-ward, not willing that any should perish, but that all should come to repentance.

II Peter 3:9

For whosoever shall do the will of God, the same is my brother, and my sister, and mother.

Mark 3:35

God's Wisdom

O the depth of the riches both of the wisdom and knowledge of God! how unsearchable are his judgments, and his ways past finding out!

Romans 11:33

Daniel answered and said, Blessed be the name of God for ever and ever: for wisdom and might are his:...He revealeth the deep and secret things: he knoweth what is in the darkness, and the light dwelleth with him.

Daniel 2:20,22

The Lord by wisdom hath founded the earth; by understanding hath he established the heavens.

Proverbs 3:19

But we preach Christ crucified, unto the Jews a stumblingblock, and unto the Greeks foolishness; But unto them which are called, both Jews and Greeks, Christ the power of God, and the wisdom of God. Because the foolishness of God is wiser than men; and the weakness of God is stronger than men.

I Corinthians 1:23-25

In whom are hid all the treasures of wisdom and knowledge.

Colossians 2:3

God's Wrath

For the wrath of God is revealed from heaven against all ungodliness and unrighteousness of men, who hold the truth in unrighteousness.

Romans 1:18

Who can stand before his indignation? and who can abide in the fierceness of his anger? his fury is poured out like fire, and the rocks are thrown down by him.

Nahum 1:6

Let no man deceive you with vain words: for because of these things cometh the wrath of God upon the children of disobedience.

Ephesians 5:6

And the third angel followed them, saying with a loud voice, If any man worship the beast and his image, and receive his mark in his forehead, or in his hand, The same shall drink of the wine of the wrath of God, which is poured out without mixture into the cup of his indignation.

Revelation 14:9,10

And I saw another sign in heaven, great and marvellous, seven angels having the seven last plagues; for in them is filled up the wrath of God.

Revelation 15:1

Jesus the
Christ....

Jesus the Christ

In the beginning was the Word, and the Word was with God, and the Word was God. The same was in the beginning with God. All things were made by him; and without him was not any thing made that was made. In him was life; and the life was the light of men.

John 1:1-4

That which was from the beginning, which we have heard, which we have seen with our eyes, which we have looked upon, and our hands have handled, of the Word of life; (For the life was manifested, and we have seen it, and bear witness, and shew unto you that eternal life, which was with the Father, and was manifested unto us;) That which we have seen and heard declare we unto you, that ye also may have fellowship with us: and truly our fellowship is with the Father, and with his Son Jesus Christ.

I John 1:1-3

And I beheld, and I heard the voice of many angels round about the throne and the beasts and the elders: and the number of them was ten thousand times ten thousand, and thousands of thousands; Saying with a loud voice, Worthy is the Lamb that was slain to receive power, and riches, and wisdom, and strength, and honour, and glory, and blessing. And every creature which is in heaven, and on the earth, and under the earth, and such as are in the sea, and all that are in them, heard I saying, Blessing, and honour, and glory, and power, be unto him that sitteth upon the throne, and unto the Lamb for ever and ever.

Revelation 5:11-13

And he hath on his vesture and on his thigh a name written, KING OF KINGS, AND LORD OF LORDS.

Revelation 19:16

Let this mind be in you, which was also in Christ Jesus: Who, being in the form of God, thought it not robbery to be equal with God: But made himself of no reputation, and took upon him the form of a servant, and was made in the likeness of men: And being found in fashion as a man, he humbled himself, and became obedient unto death, even the death of the cross.

Philippians 2:5-8

Wherefore God also hath highly exalted him, and given him a name which is above every name: That at the name of Jesus every knee should bow, of things in heaven, and things in earth, and things under the earth; And that every tongue should confess that Jesus Christ is Lord, to the glory of God the Father.

Philippians 2:9-11

Therefore the Lord himself shall give you a sign; Behold, a virgin shall conceive, and bear a son, and shall call his name Immanuel.

Isaiah 7:14

For unto us a child is born, unto us a son is given: and the government shall be upon his shoulder: and his name shall be called Wonderful, Counsellor, The mighty God, The everlasting Father, The Prince of Peace.

Isaiah 9:6

And, behold, thou shalt conceive in thy womb, and bring forth a son, and shalt call his name JESUS. He shall be great, and shall be called the Son of the Highest: and the Lord God shall give unto him the throne of his father David: And he shall reign over the house of Jacob for ever; and of his kingdom there shall be no end.

Luke 1:31-33

But while he thought on these things, behold, the angel of the Lord appeared unto him in a dream, saying, Joseph, thou son of David, fear not to take unto thee Mary thy wife: for that which is conceived in her is of the Holy Ghost. And she shall bring forth a son, and thou shalt call his name JESUS: for he shall save his people from their sins.

Matthew 1:20,21

And she brought forth her firstborn son, and wrapped him in swaddling clothes, and laid him in a manger; because there was no room for them in the inn.

Luke 2:7

For God so loved the world, that he gave his only begotten Son, that whosoever believeth in him should not perish, but have everlasting life.

John 3:16

And the Word was made flesh, and dwelt among us, (and we beheld his glory, the glory as of the only begotten of the Father,) full of grace and truth.

John 1:14

For unto you is born this day in the city of David a Saviour, which is Christ the Lord.

Luke 2:11

Then took he him up in his arms, and blessed God, and said, Lord, now lettest thou thy servant depart in peace, according to thy word: For mine eyes have seen thy salvation, Which thou hast prepared before the face of all people; A light to lighten the Gentiles, and the glory of thy people Israel.

Luke 2:28-32

And he said unto them, How is it that ye sought me? wist ye not that I must be about my Father's business?

Luke 2:49

John answered, saying unto them all, I indeed baptize you with water; but one mightier than I cometh, the latchet of whose shoes I am not worthy to unloose: he shall baptize you with the Holy Ghost and with fire.

Luke 3:16

And I knew him not: but he that sent me to baptize with water, the same said unto me, Upon whom thou shalt see the Spirit descending, and remaining on him, the same is he which baptizeth with the Holy Ghost. And I saw, and bare record that this is the Son of God.

John 1:33,34

And Jesus, when he was baptized, went up straightway out of the water: and, lo, the heavens were opened unto him, and he saw the Spirit of God descending like a dove, and lighting upon him: And lo a voice from heaven, saying, This is my beloved Son, in whom I am well pleased.

Matthew 3:16,17

But I say unto you, That in this place is one greater than the temple. ... For the Son of man is Lord even of the sabbath day.

Matthew 12:6,8

And Simon Peter answered and said, Thou art the Christ, the Son of the living God. And Jesus answered and said unto him, Blessed art thou, Simon Bar-jona: for flesh and blood hath not revealed it unto thee, but my Father which is in heaven. And I say also unto thee, That thou art Peter, and upon this rock I will build my church; and the gates of hell shall not prevail against it.

Matthew 16:16-18

For the Son of man is come to save that which was lost.

Matthew 18:11

Even as the Son of man came not to be ministered unto, but to minister, and to give his life a ransom for many.

Matthew 20:28

Then spake Jesus again unto them, saying, I am the light of the world: he that followeth me shall not walk in darkness, but shall have the light of life.

John 8:12

Then said Jesus unto them again, Verily, verily, I say unto you, I am the door of the sheep. All that ever came before me are thieves and robbers: but the sheep did not hear them. I am the door: by me if any man enter in, he shall be saved, and shall go in and out, and find pasture.

John 10:7-9

Neither is there salvation in any other: for there is none other name under heaven given among men, whereby we must be saved.

Acts 4:12

And Jesus came and spake unto them, saying, All power is given unto me in heaven and in earth.

Matthew 28:18

Neither be ye called masters: for one is your Master, even Christ.

Matthew 23:10

For God sent not his Son into the world to condemn the world; but that the world through him might be saved.

John 3:17

Heaven and earth shall pass away, but my words shall not pass away.

Matthew 24:35

And have ye not read this scripture; The stone which the builders rejected is become the head of the corner.

Mark 12:10

The Spirit of the Lord is upon me, because he hath anointed me to preach the gospel to the poor; he hath sent me to heal the brokenhearted, to preach deliverance to the captives, and recovering of sight to the blind, to set at liberty them that are bruised, To preach the acceptable year of the Lord. . . . And he began to say unto them, This day is this scripture fulfilled in your ears.

Luke 4:18,19,21

And devils also came out of many, crying out, and saying, Thou art Christ the Son of God. And he rebuking them suffered them not to speak: for they knew that he was Christ.

Luke 4:41

For the Son of man is not come to

destroy men's lives, but to save them.

Luke 9:56

But whosoever drinketh of the water that I shall give him shall never thirst; but the water that I shall give him shall be in him a well of water springing up into everlasting life.

John 4:14

And many more believed because of his own word; And said unto the woman, Now we believe, not because of thy saying: for we have heard him ourselves, and know that this is indeed the Christ, the Saviour of the world.

John 4:41,42

Verily, verily, I say unto you, He that heareth my word, and believeth on him that sent me, hath everlasting life, and shall not come into condemnation; but is passed from death unto life.

John 5:24

And Jesus said unto them, I am the bread of life: he that cometh to me shall never hunger; and he that believeth on me shall never thirst.

John 6:35

... I am come that they might have life, and that they might have it more abundantly.

John 10:10

I am the good shepherd: the good shepherd giveth his life for the sheep.

John 10:11

My sheep hear my voice, and I know them, and they follow me: And I give unto them eternal life; and they shall never perish, neither shall any man pluck them out of my hand. My Father, which gave them me, is greater than all; and no man is able to pluck them out of my Father's hand. I and my Father are one.

John 10:27-30

Jesus said unto her, I am the resurrection, and the life: he that believeth in me, though he were dead, yet shall he live: And whosoever liveth and believeth in me shall never die. Believest thou this?

John 11:25,26

Now is my soul troubled; and what shall I say? Father, save me from this hour: but for this cause came I unto this hour. Father, glorify thy name. Then came there a voice from heaven, saying, I have both glorified it, and will glorify it again.

John 12:27,28

Jesus saith unto him, I am the way, the truth, and the life: no man cometh unto the Father, but by me.

John 14:6

Jesus saith unto him, Have I been so long time with you, and yet hast thou not known me, Philip? he that hath seen me hath seen the Father; and how sayest thou then, Shew us the Father? Believest thou not that I am in the

Father, and the Father in me? the words that I speak unto you I speak not of myself: but the Father that dwelleth in me, he doeth the works.

John 14:9,10

I am the true vine, and my Father is the husbandman.

John 15:1

Abide in me, and I in you. As the branch cannot bear fruit of itself, except it abide in the vine; no more can ye, except ye abide in me. I am the vine, ye are the branches: He that abideth in me, and I in him, the same bringeth forth much fruit: for without me ye can do nothing.

John 15:4,5

As the Father hath loved me, so have I loved you: continue ye in my love.

John 15:9

For the Father himself loveth you, because ye have loved me, and have believed that I came out from God. I came forth from the Father, and am come into the world: again, I leave the world, and go to the Father.

John 16:27,28

These things I have spoken unto you, that in me ye might have peace. In the world ye shall have tribulation: but be of good cheer; I have overcome the world.

John 16:33

And now, O Father, glorify thou me

with thine own self with the glory which I had with thee before the world was.

John 17:5

And many other signs truly did Jesus in the presence of his disciples, which are not written in this book: But these are written, that ye might believe that Jesus is the Christ, the Son of God; and that believing ye might have life through his name.

John 20:30,31

And there are also many other things which Jesus did, the which, if they should be written every one, I suppose that even the world itself could not contain the books that should be written. Amen.

John 21:25

In whom we have redemption through his blood, the forgiveness of sins, according to the riches of his grace.

Ephesians 1:7

But when he saw the multitudes, he was moved with compassion on them, because they fainted, and were scattered abroad, as sheep having no shepherd.

Matthew 9:36

And when I saw him, I fell at his feet as dead. And he laid his right hand upon me, saying unto me, Fear not; I am the first and the last: I am he that liveth, and was dead; and, behold, I am alive for evermore, Amen; and have the keys of hell and of death.

Revelation 1:17,18

... for he is Lord of lords, and King of kings: and they that are with him are called, and chosen, and faithful.

Revelation 17:14

And he is the head of the body, the church: who is the beginning, the firstborn from the dead; that in all things he might have the preeminence.

Colossians 1:18

I Jesus have sent mine angel to testify unto you these things in the churches. I am the root and the offspring of David, and the bright and morning star.

Revelation 22:16

For ye know the grace of our Lord Jesus Christ, that, though he was rich, yet for your sakes he became poor, that ye through his poverty might be rich.

II Corinthians 8:9

For whether is greater, he that sitteth at meat, or he that serveth? is not he that sitteth at meat? but I am among you as he that serveth.

Luke 22:27

That as sin hath reigned unto death, even so might grace reign through righteousness unto eternal life by Jesus Christ our Lord.

Romans 5:21

Take my yoke upon you, and learn of me; for I am meek and lowly in heart: and ye shall find rest unto your souls.

Matthew 11:29

And ye know that he was manifested to take away our sins; and in him is no sin.

I John 3:5

...For this purpose the Son of God was manifested, that he might destroy the works of the devil.

I John 3:8

For both he that sanctifieth and they who are sanctified are all of one: for which cause he is not ashamed to call them brethren.

Hebrews 2:11

Looking unto Jesus the author and finisher of our faith; who for the joy that was set before him endured the cross, despising the shame, and is set down at the right hand of the throne of God.

Hebrews 12:2

Which in his times he shall shew, who is the blessed and only Potentate, the King of kings, and Lord of lords.

I Timothy 6:15

And I saw heaven opened, and behold a white horse; and he that sat upon him was called Faithful and True, and in righteousness he doth judge and make war.

Revelation 19:11

The next day John seeth Jesus coming unto him, and saith, Behold the Lamb of God, which taketh away the sin of the world.

John 1:29

Many of the people therefore, when they heard this saying, said, Of a truth this is the Prophet.

John 7:40

These words spake Jesus, and lifted up his eyes to heaven, and said, Father, the hour is come; glorify thy Son, that thy Son also may glorify thee.

John 17:1

I have glorified thee on the earth: I have finished the work which thou gavest me to do.

John 17:4

And he answered and said, He that dippeth his hand with me in the dish, the same shall betray me.

Matthew 26:23

Yea, mine own familiar friend, in whom I trusted, which did eat of my bread, hath lifted up his heel against me.

Psalm 41:9

And he was withdrawn from them about a stone's cast, and kneeled down, and prayed, Saying, Father, if thou be willing, remove this cup from me: nevertheless not my will, but thine, be done.

Luke 22:41,42

And being in an agony he prayed more earnestly: and his sweat was as it were great drops of blood falling down to the ground.

Luke 22:44

But all this was done, that the scriptures of the prophets might be fulfilled. Then all the disciples forsook him, and fled.

Matthew 26:56

When the morning was come, all the chief priests and elders of the people took counsel against Jesus to put him to death: And when they had bound him, they led him away, and delivered him to Pontius Pilate the governor.

Matthew 27:1,2

...Again the high priest asked him, and said unto him, Art thou the Christ, the Son of the Blessed? And Jesus said, I am: and ye shall see the Son of man sitting on the right hand of power, and coming in the clouds of heaven.

Mark 14:61,62

And when they were come to the place, which is called Calvary, there they crucified him, and the malefactors, one on the right hand, and the other on the left.

Luke 23:33

And when Jesus had cried with a loud voice, he said, Father, into thy hands I commend my spirit: and having said thus, he gave up the ghost.

Luke 23:46

He is despised and rejected of men; a man of sorrows, and acquainted with grief: and we hid as it were our faces from him; he was despised, and we esteemed him not. Surely he hath borne our griefs, and carried our sorrows: yet we did esteem him stricken, smitten of God, and afflicted. But he was wounded for our transgressions, he was bruised for our iniquities: the chastisement of our peace was upon him; and with his stripes we are healed. All we like sheep have gone astray; we have turned every one to his own way; and the Lord hath laid on him the iniquity of us all.

Isaiah 53:3-6

And the angel answered and said unto the women, Fear not ye: for I know that ye seek Jesus, which was crucified. He is not here: for he is risen, as he said. Come, see the place where the Lord lay.

Matthew 28:5,6

And as they thus spake, Jesus himself stood in the midst of them, and saith unto them, Peace be unto you. But they were terrified and affrighted, and supposed that they had seen a spirit. And he said unto them, Why are ye troubled? and why do thoughts arise in your hearts? Behold my hands and my feet, that it is I myself: handle me, and see; for a spirit hath not flesh and bones, as ye see me have. And when he had thus spoken, he shewed them his hands and his feet. And while they yet believed not for joy, and wondered, he said unto them, Have ye here any meat? And they gave him a piece of a broiled fish, and of an honeycomb. And he took it, and did eat before them.

Luke 24:36-43

To whom also he shewed himself alive after his passion by many infallible proofs, being seen of them forty days, and speaking of the things pertaining to the kingdom of God.

Acts 1:3

And to wait for his Son from heaven, whom he raised from the dead, even Jesus, which delivered us from the wrath to come.

I Thessalonians 1:10

Be it known unto you all, and to all the people of Israel, that by the name of Jesus Christ of Nazareth, whom ye crucified, whom God raised from the dead.

Acts 4:10

And with great power gave the apostles witness of the resurrection of the Lord Jesus: and great grace was upon them all.

Acts 4:33

Blessed be the God and Father of our Lord Jesus Christ, which according to his abundant mercy hath begotten us again unto a lively hope by the resurrection of Jesus Christ from the dead.

I Peter 1:3

. . . whereof he hath given assurance unto all men, in that he hath raised him from the dead.

Acts 17:31

Therefore we are buried with him by baptism into death: that like as Christ was raised up from the dead by the glory of the Father, even so we also should walk in newness of life.

Romans 6:4

But if the Spirit of him that raised up Jesus from the dead dwell in you, he that raised up Christ from the dead shall also quicken your mortal bodies by his Spirit that dwelleth in you.

Romans 8:11

Who is he that condemneth? It is Christ that died, yea rather, that is risen again, who is even at the right hand of God, who also maketh intercession for us.

Romans 8:34

And God hath both raised up the Lord, and will also raise up us by his own power.

I Corinthians 6:14

For I delivered unto you first of all that which I also received, how that Christ died for our sins according to the scriptures; And that he was buried, and that he rose again the third day according to the scriptures: And that he was seen of Cephas, then of the twelve: After that, he was seen of above five hundred brethren at once; of whom the greater part remain unto this present, but some are fallen asleep. After that, he was seen of James; then of all the apostles. And last of all he was seen of me also, as of one born out of due time.

I Corinthians 15:3-8

And when he had spoken these things, while they beheld, he was taken up; and a cloud received him out of their sight. And while they looked stedfastly toward heaven as he went up, behold, two men stood by them in white apparel; Which also said, Ye men of Galilee, why stand ye gazing up into heaven? this same Jesus, which is taken up from you into heaven, shall so come in like manner as ye have seen him go into heaven.

Acts 1:9-11

... I go to prepare a place for you. And if I go and prepare a place for you, I will come again, and receive you unto myself; that where I am, there ye may be also.

John 14:2,3

For the Son of man shall come in the glory of his Father with his angels; and then he shall reward every man according to his works.

Matthew 16:27

For as the lightning cometh out of the east, and shineth even unto the west; so shall also the coming of the Son of man be.

Matthew 24:27

But as the days of Noe were, so shall also the coming of the Son of man be. For as in the days that were before the flood they were eating and drinking, marrying and giving in marriage, until the day that Noe entered into the ark, And knew not until the flood came, and took them all away; so shall also the coming of the Son of man be. Then shall two be in the field; the one shall be taken, and the other left. Two women shall be grinding at the mill; the one shall be taken, and the other left. Watch therefore: for ye know not what hour your Lord doth come.

Matthew 24:37-42

Therefore be ye also ready: for in such an hour as ye think not the Son of man cometh.

Matthew 24:44

But of that day and hour knoweth no man, no, not the angels of heaven, but my Father only.

Matthew 24:36

When the Son of man shall come in his glory, and all the holy angels with him, then shall he sit upon the throne of his glory.

Matthew 25:31

Jesus saith unto him, Thou hast said: nevertheless I say unto you, Hereafter shall ye see the Son of man sitting on the right hand of power, and coming in the clouds of heaven.

Matthew 26:64

For whosoever shall be ashamed of me and of my words, of him shall the Son of man be ashamed, when he shall come in his own glory, and in his Father's, and of the holy angels.

Luke 9:26

For the Lord himself shall descend from heaven with a shout, with the voice of the archangel, and with the trump of God: and the dead in Christ shall rise first: Then we which are alive and remain shall be caught up together with them in the clouds, to meet the Lord in the air: and so shall we ever be with the Lord.

I Thessalonians 4:16,17

For yourselves know perfectly that the day of the Lord so cometh as a thief in the night. For when they shall say, Peace and safety; then sudden destruction cometh upon them, as travail upon a woman with child; and they shall not escape.

I Thessalonians 5:2,3

So Christ was once offered to bear the sins of many; and unto them that look for him shall he appear the second time without sin unto salvation.

Hebrews 9:28

He which testifieth these things saith, Surely I come quickly. Amen. Even so, come, Lord Jesus.

Revelation 22:20

The Holy
Spirit....

The Holy Spirit

And I will pray the Father, and he shall give you another Comforter, that he may abide with you for ever; Even the Spirit of truth; whom the world cannot receive, because it seeth him not, neither knoweth him: but ye know him; for he dwelleth with you, and shall be in you.

John 14:16,17

But the Comforter, which is the Holy Ghost, whom the Father will send in my name, he shall teach you all things, and bring all things to your remembrance, whatsoever I have said unto you.

John 14:26

But when the Comforter is come, whom I will send unto you from the Father, even the Spirit of truth, which proceedeth from the Father, he shall testify of me.

John 15:26

Howbeit when he, the Spirit of truth, is come, he will guide you into all truth: for he shall not speak of himself; but whatsoever he shall hear, that shall he speak: and he will shew you things to come. He shall glorify me: for he shall receive of mine, and shall shew it unto you.

John 16:13,14

Jesus answered, Verily, verily, I say unto thee, Except a man be born of water and of the Spirit, he cannot enter into the kingdom of God. That which is born of the flesh is flesh; and that which is born of the Spirit is spirit. Marvel not that I said unto thee, Ye must be born again. The wind bloweth where it listeth, and thou hearest the sound thereof, but canst not tell whence it cometh, and whither it goeth: so is every one that is born of the Spirit.

John 3:5-8

And when he is come, he will reprove the world of sin, and of righteousness, and of judgment.

John 16:8

And when the day of Pentecost was fully come, they were all with one accord in one place. And suddenly there came a sound from heaven as of a rushing mighty wind, and it filled all the house where they were sitting. And there appeared unto them cloven tongues like as of fire, and it sat upon each of them. And they were all filled with the Holy Ghost, and began to speak with other tongues, as the Spirit gave them utterance.

Acts 2:1-4

For as many as are led by the Spirit of God, they are the sons of God. For ye have not received the spirit of bondage again to fear; but ye have received the Spirit of adoption, whereby we cry, Abba, Father. The Spirit itself beareth witness with our spirit, that we are the children of God.

Romans 8:14-16

And God, which knoweth the hearts, bare them witness, giving them the Holy Ghost, even as he did unto us.

Acts 15:8

Ye stiffnecked and uncircumcised in heart and ears, ye do always resist the Holy Ghost: as your fathers did, so do ye.

Acts 7:51

Then had the churches rest throughout all Judaea and Galilee and Samaria, and were edified; and walking in the fear of the Lord, and in the comfort of the Holy Ghost, were multiplied.

Acts 9:31

As they ministered to the Lord, and fasted, the Holy Ghost said, Separate me Barnabas and Saul for the work whereunto I have called them. And when they had fasted and prayed, and laid their hands on them, they sent them away. So they, being sent forth by the Holy Ghost, departed unto Seleucia; and from thence they sailed to Cyprus.

Acts 13:2-4

Then Saul, (who also is called Paul,) filled with the Holy Ghost, set his eyes on him.

Acts 13:9

And when they had prayed, the place was shaken where they were assembled together; and they were all filled with the Holy Ghost, and they spake the word of God with boldness.

Acts 4:31

If ye then, being evil, know how to give good gifts unto your children: how much more shall your heavenly Father give the Holy Spirit to them that ask him?

Luke 11:13

But the manifestation of the Spirit is given to every man to profit withal. For to one is given by the Spirit the word of wisdom; to another the word of knowledge by the same Spirit; To another faith by the same Spirit; to another the gifts of healing by the same Spirit; To another the working of miracles; to another prophecy; to another discerning of spirits; to another divers kinds of tongues; to another the interpretation of tongues: But all these worketh that one and the selfsame Spirit, dividing to every man severally as he will.

I Corinthians 12:7-11

Now when the apostles which were at Jerusalem heard that Samaria had received the word of God, they sent unto them Peter and John: Who, when they were come down, prayed for them, that they might receive the Holy Ghost: (For as yet he was fallen upon none of them: only they were baptized in the name of the Lord Jesus.) Then laid they their hands on them, and they received the Holy Ghost.

Acts 8:14-17

But the fruit of the Spirit is love, joy, peace, longsuffering, gentleness, goodness, faith, Meekness, temperance: against such there is no law. And they that are Christ's have crucified the flesh with the affections and lusts. If we live in the Spirit, let us also walk in the Spirit.

Galatians 5:22-25

Likewise the Spirit also helpeth our infirmities: for we know not what we should pray for as we ought: but the Spirit itself maketh intercession for us with groanings which cannot be uttered.

Romans 8:26

But after that the kindness and love of God our Saviour toward man appeared, Not by works of righteousness which we have done, but according to his mercy he saved us, by the washing of regeneration, and renewing of the Holy Ghost; Which he shed on us abundantly through Jesus Christ our Saviour.

Titus 3:4-6

Know ye not that ye are the temple of God, and that the Spirit of God dwelleth in you?

I Corinthians 3:16

What? know ye not that your body is the temple of the Holy Ghost which is in you, which ye have of God, and ye are not your own?

I Corinthians 6:19

But when they shall lead you, and deliver you up, take no thought beforehand what ye shall speak, neither do ye premeditate: but whatsoever shall be given you in that hour, that speak ye: for it is not ye that speak, but the Holy Ghost.

Mark 13:11

For the kingdom of God is not meat and drink; but righteousness, and peace, and joy in the Holy Ghost.

Romans 14:17

Now the God of hope fill you with all joy and peace in believing, that ye may abound in hope, through the power of the Holy Ghost.

Romans 15:13

In whom ye also trusted, after that ye heard the word of truth, the gospel of your salvation: in whom also after that ye believed, ye were sealed with that holy Spirit of promise, Which is the earnest of our inheritance until the redemption of the purchased possession, unto the praise of his glory.

Ephesians 1:13,14

But as it is written, Eye hath not seen, nor ear heard, neither have entered into the heart of man, the things which God hath prepared for them that love him. But God hath revealed them unto us by his Spirit: for the

Spirit searcheth all things, yea, the deep things of God. For what man knoweth the things of a man, save the spirit of man which is in him? even so the things of God knoweth no man, but the Spirit of God. Now we have received, not the spirit of the world, but the spirit which is of God; that we might know the things that are freely given to us of God. Which things also we speak, not in the words which man's wisdom teacheth, but which the Holy Ghost teacheth; comparing spiritual things with spiritual.

I Corinthians 2:9-13

There is therefore now no condemnation to them which are in Christ Jesus, who walk not after the flesh, but after the Spirit.

Romans 8:1

And this is his commandment, That we should believe on the name of his Son Jesus Christ, and love one another, as he gave us commandment. And he that keepeth his commandments dwelleth in him, and he in him. And hereby we know that he abideth in us, by the Spirit which he hath given us.

I John 3:23,24

For he that soweth to his flesh shall of the flesh reap corruption; but he that soweth to the Spirit shall of the Spirit reap life everlasting.

Galatians 6:8

This I say then, Walk in the Spirit, and ye shall not fulfil the lust of the flesh. For the flesh lusteth against the Spirit, and the Spirit against the flesh: and these are contrary the one to the other: so that ye cannot do the things that ye would. But if ye be led of the Spirit, ye are not under the law.

Galatians 5:16-18

For they that are after the flesh do mind the things of the flesh; but they that are after the Spirit the things of the Spirit. For to be carnally minded is death; but to be spiritually minded is life and peace.

Romans 8:5,6

But ye are not in the flesh, but in the Spirit, if so be that the Spirit of God dwell in you. Now if any man have not the Spirit of Christ, he is none of his. And if Christ be in you, the body is dead because of sin; but the Spirit is life because of righteousness. But if the Spirit of him that raised up Jesus from the dead dwell in you, he that raised up Christ from the dead shall also quicken your mortal bodies by his Spirit that dwelleth in you.

Romans 8:9-11

But we all, with open face beholding as in a glass the glory of the Lord, are changed into the same image from glory to glory, even as by the Spirit of the Lord.

II Corinthians 3:18

And such were some of you: but ye are washed, but ye are sanctified, but ye are justified in the name of the Lord Jesus, and by the Spirit of our God.

I Corinthians 6:11

Wherefore I give you to understand, that no man speaking by the Spirit of God calleth Jesus accursed: and that no man can say that Jesus is the Lord, but by the Holy Ghost.

I Corinthians 12:3

For through him we both have access by one Spirit unto the Father.

Ephesians 2:18

And take the helmet of salvation, and the sword of the Spirit, which is the word of God: Praying always with all prayer and supplication in the Spirit, and watching thereunto with all perseverance and supplication for all saints.

Ephesians 6:17,18

And hope maketh not ashamed; because the love of God is shed abroad in our hearts by the Holy Ghost which is given unto us.

Romans 5:5

And be not drunk with wine, wherein is excess; but be filled with the Spirit.

Ephesians 5:18

For by one Spirit are we all baptized into one body, whether we be Jews or Gentiles, whether we be bond or free; and have been all made to drink into one Spirit.

I Corinthians 12:13

And my speech and my preaching was not with enticing words of man's wisdom, but in demonstration of the Spirit and of power.

I Corinthians 2:4

And we are his witnesses of these things; and so is also the Holy Ghost, whom God hath given to them that obey him.

Acts 5:32

Now he which stablisheth us with you in Christ, and hath anointed us, is God; Who hath also sealed us, and given the earnest of the Spirit in our hearts.

II Corinthians 1:21,22

For our gospel came not unto you in word only, but also in power, and in the Holy Ghost, and in much assurance; as ye know what manner of men we were among you for your sake. And ye became followers of us, and of the Lord, having received the word in much affliction, with joy of the Holy Ghost.

I Thessalonians 1:5,6

That good thing which was committed unto thee keep by the Holy Ghost which dwelleth in us.

II Timothy 1:14

Which in other ages was not made known unto the sons of men, as it is now revealed unto his holy apostles and prophets by the Spirit.

Ephesians 3:5

THE HOLY SPIRIT

For this cause I bow my knees unto the Father of our Lord Jesus Christ, Of whom the whole family in heaven and earth is named, That he would grant you, according to the riches of his glory, to be strengthened with might by his Spirit in the inner man.

Ephesians 3:14-16

Beloved, if God so loved us, we ought also to love one another. No man hath seen God at any time. If we love one another, God dwelleth in us, and his love is perfected in us. Hereby know we that we dwell in him, and he in us, because he hath given us of his Spirit.

I John 4:11-13

And it shall come to pass in the last days, saith God, I will pour out of my Spirit upon all flesh: and your sons and your daughters shall prophesy, and your young men shall see visions, and your old men shall dream dreams.

Acts 2:17

And grieve not the holy Spirit of God, whereby ye are sealed unto the day of redemption.

Ephesians 4:30

Quench not the Spirit.

I Thessalonians 5:19

Bible Topics With Scripture....

Amazing Grace

For by grace are ye saved through faith; and that not of yourselves: it is the gift of God: Not of works, lest any man should boast.

Ephesians 2:8,9

For the grace of God that bringeth salvation hath appeared to all men.

Titus 2:11

Let us therefore come boldly unto the throne of grace, that we may obtain mercy, and find grace to help in time of need.

Hebrews 4:16

For the Lord God is a sun and shield: the Lord will give grace and glory: no good thing will he withhold from them that walk uprightly.

Psalm 84:11

Therefore being justified by faith, we have peace with God through our Lord Jesus Christ: By whom also we have access by faith into this grace wherein we stand, and rejoice in hope of the glory of God.

Romans 5:1,2

But not as the offence, so also is the free gift. For if through the offence of one many be dead, much more the grace of God, and the gift by grace, which is by one man, Jesus Christ, hath abounded unto many.

Romans 5:15

John bare witness of him, and cried,

saying, This was he of whom I spake, He that cometh after me is preferred before me: for he was before me. And of his fulness have all we received, and grace for grace.

John 1:15,16

And God is able to make all grace abound toward you; that ye, always having all sufficiency in all things, may abound to every good work.

II Corinthians 9:8

For this thing I besought the Lord thrice, that it might depart from me. And he said unto me, My grace is sufficient for thee: for my strength is made perfect in weakness. Most gladly therefore will I rather glory in my infirmities, that the power of Christ may rest upon me.

II Corinthians 12:8,9

For the law was given by Moses, but grace and truth came by Jesus Christ.

John 1:17

Additional Scripture References

Gen. 6:8; Deut. 7:6-8; Prov. 3:34; Acts 15:11; 20:24; Rom. 1:1-7; 3:23,24; 5:18-21; 6:14; 11:1-6; I Cor. 10:13; Eph. 1:5-7; 2:4-8; 3:7,8; 4:7; I Tim. 1:14; Titus 3:3-7; I Pet. 4:10

Angels

Thou, even thou, art Lord alone; thou hast made heaven, the heaven of heavens, with all their host, the earth, and all things that are therein, the seas, and all that is therein, and thou preservest them all; and the host of heaven worshippeth thee.

Nehemiah 9:6

Are they not all ministering spirits, sent forth to minister for them who shall be heirs of salvation?

Hebrews 1:14

The angel of the Lord encampeth round about them that fear him, and delivereth them.

Psalm 34:7

For he shall give his angels charge over thee, to keep thee in all thy ways. They shall bear thee up in their hands, lest thou dash thy foot against a stone.

Psalm 91:11,12

But ye are come unto mount Sion, and unto the city of the living God, the heavenly Jerusalem, and to an innumerable company of angels.

Hebrews 12:22

Who is gone into heaven, and is on the right hand of God; angels and authorities and powers being made subject unto him.

I Peter 3:22

Bless the Lord, ye his angels, that excel in strength, that do his commandments, hearkening unto the voice of his word. Bless ye the Lord, all ye his hosts; ye ministers of his, that do his pleasure.

Psalm 103:20,21

Likewise, I say unto you, there is joy in the presence of the angels of God over one sinner that repenteth.

Luke 15:10

Thinkest thou that I cannot now pray to my Father, and he shall presently give me more than twelve legions of angels?

Matthew 26:53

And Jacob went on his way, and the angels of God met him. And when Jacob saw them, he said, This is God's host: and he called the name of that place Mahanaim.

Genesis 32:1,2

Additional Scripture References

Josh. 5:13-15; I Kin. 19:5-8; 22:19;
I Chr. 21:15; Ps. 104:4; Dan. 6:22; 9:21,22;
10:10-15; Matt. 1:20-24; 16:27; 18:10; 24:30,31;
Luke 1:26-38; 2:8-14; Acts 5:19; 8:26;
12:8-11; 27:4-35; Col. 1:16; II Pet. 2:4-11;
Rev. 5:11,12

Anxiety - Worldly Care

Be careful for nothing; but in every thing by prayer and supplication with thanksgiving let your requests be made known unto God. And the peace of God, which passeth all understanding, shall keep your hearts and minds through Christ Jesus.

Philippians 4:6,7

Cast thy burden upon the Lord, and he shall sustain thee: he shall never suffer the righteous to be moved.

Psalm 55:22

Thou therefore endure hardness, as a good soldier of Jesus Christ. No man that warreth entangleth himself with the affairs of this life; that he may please him who hath chosen him to be a soldier.

II Timothy 2:3,4

He that dwelleth in the secret place of the most High shall abide under the shadow of the Almighty.

Psalm 91:1

For he shall give his angels charge over thee, to keep thee in all thy ways. They shall bear thee up in their hands, lest thou dash thy foot against a stone.

Psalm 91:11,12

The Lord preserveth the simple: I was brought low, and he helped me. Return unto thy rest, O my soul; for the Lord hath dealt bountifully with thee. For thou hast delivered my soul from death, mine eyes from tears, and my feet from falling.

Psalm 116:6-8

Take my yoke upon you, and learn of me; for I am meek and lowly in heart: and ye shall find rest unto your souls.

Matthew 11:29

When thou liest down, thou shalt not be afraid: yea, thou shalt lie down, and thy sleep shall be sweet.

Proverbs 3:24

Commit thy works unto the Lord, and thy thoughts shall be established.

Proverbs 16:3

Humble yourselves therefore under the mighty hand of God, that he may exalt you in due time: Casting all your care upon him; for he careth for you.

I Peter 5:6,7

Additional Scripture References

Ps. 17:8,9; 23; 27:1; 37:5; 56:9; 57:1-3; 63:7; 94:12,13; 112:7; Is. 32:17; Matt. 6:25-34; 13:18-23; Mark 4:19; Luke 12:22-31; Phil. 4:8; Heb. 13:5,6

Armor of God

Put on the whole armour of God, that ye may be able to stand against the wiles of the devil.

Ephesians 6:11

The night is far spent, the day is at hand: let us therefore cast off the works of darkness, and let us put on the armour of light.

Romans 13:12

By the word of truth, by the power of God, by the armour of righteousness on the right hand and on the left.

II Corinthians 6:7

(For the weapons of our warfare are not carnal, but mighty through God to the pulling down of strong holds;).

II Corinthians 10:4

For he put on righteousness as a breastplate, and an helmet of salvation upon his head; and he put on the garments of vengeance for clothing, and was clad with zeal as a cloak.

Isaiah 59:17

But let us, who are of the day, be sober, putting on the breastplate of faith and love; and for an helmet, the hope of salvation.

I Thessalonians 5:8

After these things the word of the Lord came unto Abram in a vision, saying, Fear not,

Abram: I am thy shield, and thy exceeding great reward.

Genesis 15:1

But thou, O Lord, art a shield for me; my glory, and the lifter up of mine head.

Psalm 3:3

He shall cover thee with his feathers, and under his wings shalt thou trust: his truth shall be thy shield and buckler.

Psalm 91:4

Additional Scripture References

Prov. 18:10; Is. 49:2; Hab. 3:19; II Cor. 1:24; Eph. 6:13-18; I Tim. 1:18,19; II Tim. 2:21; Heb. 4:12; 13:5,6; Rev. 12:11; 19:15

Assurance of Salvation

I, even I, am he that blotteth out thy transgressions for mine own sake, and will not remember thy sins.

Isaiah 43:25

As far as the east is from the west, so far hath he removed our transgressions from us.

Psalm 103:12

I have blotted out, as a thick cloud, thy transgressions, and, as a cloud, thy sins: return unto me; for I have redeemed thee.

Isaiah 44:22

For by grace are ye saved through faith; and that not of yourselves: it is the gift of God: Not of works, lest any man should boast.

Ephesians 2:8,9

In whom ye also trusted, after that ye heard the word of truth, the gospel of your salvation: in whom also after that ye believed, ye were sealed with that holy Spirit of promise, Which is the earnest of our inheritance until the redemption of the purchased possession, unto the praise of his glory.

Ephesians 1:13,14

My sheep hear my voice, and I know them, and they follow me: And I give unto them eternal life; and they shall never perish, neither shall any man pluck them out of my hand. My Father, which gave them me, is greater than all;

and no man is able to pluck them out of my Father's hand.

John 10:27-29

Being confident of this very thing, that he which hath begun a good work in you will perform it until the day of Jesus Christ.

Philippians 1:6

All that the Father giveth me shall come to me; and him that cometh to me I will in no wise cast out.

John 6:37

That if thou shalt confess with thy mouth the Lord Jesus, and shalt believe in thine heart that God hath raised him from the dead, thou shalt be saved. For with the heart man believeth unto righteousness; and with the mouth confession is made unto salvation.

Romans 10:9,10

Additional Scripture References

Nah. 1:7; Luke 23:39-43; John 5:24; 8:51; Rom. 8:14-17; 8:38,39; II Cor. 1:21,22; Eph. 4:30; I Thes. 1:4; II Tim. 2:19; Heb. 10:12-18; I Pet. 1:2; I Jn. 2:19; 4:6; 5:13

The Atonement

For this is my blood of the new testament, which is shed for many for the remission of sins.

Matthew 26:28

Whom God hath set forth to be a propitiation through faith in his blood, to declare his righteousness for the remission of sins that are past, through the forbearance of God.

Romans 3:25

For he hath made him to be sin for us, who knew no sin; that we might be made the righteousness of God in him.

II Corinthians 5:21

Who gave himself for our sins, that he might deliver us from this present evil world, according to the will of God and our Father.

Galatians 1:4

In whom we have redemption through his blood, the forgiveness of sins, according to the riches of his grace.

Ephesians 1:7

And walk in love, as Christ also hath loved us, and hath given himself for us an offering and a sacrifice to God for a sweet-smelling savour.

Ephesians 5:2

Who his own self bare our sins in his own body on the tree, that we, being dead to sins, should live unto righteousness: by whose stripes ye were healed.

I Peter 2:24

For Christ also hath once suffered for sins, the just for the unjust, that he might bring us to God, being put to death in the flesh, but quickened by the Spirit.

I Peter 3:18

And he is the propitiation for our sins: and not for ours only, but also for the sins of the whole world.

I John 2:2

And from Jesus Christ, who is the faithful witness, and the first begotten of the dead, and the prince of the kings of the earth. Unto him that loved us, and washed us from our sins in his own blood.

Revelation 1:5

But this man, after he had offered one sacrifice for sins for ever, sat down on the right hand of God.

Hebrews 10:12

Additional Scripture References

Is. 53:5; Rom. 5:6-11; I Cor. 15:3; Eph. 2:16; Col. 1:20-22; Heb. 9:14,15; I Jn. 4:10

The Bible -
Inspired Word of God

All scripture is given by inspiration of God, and is profitable for doctrine, for reproof, for correction, for instruction in righteousness.

II Timothy 3:16

Knowing this first, that no prophecy of the scripture is of any private interpretation. For the prophecy came not in old time by the will of man: but holy men of God spake as they were moved by the Holy Ghost.

II Peter 1:20,21

For whatsoever things were written aforetime were written for our learning, that we through patience and comfort of the scriptures might have hope.

Romans 15:4

And I heard a voice from heaven saying unto me, Write, Blessed are the dead which die in the Lord from henceforth: Yea, saith the Spirit, that they may rest from their labours; and their works do follow them.

Revelation 14:13

Moreover the Lord said unto me, Take thee a great roll, and write in it with a man's pen concerning Maher-shalal-hash-baz. And I took unto me faithful witnesses to record, Uriah the priest, and Zechariah the son of Jeberechiah.

Isaiah 8:1,2

Men and brethren, this scripture must needs have been fulfilled, which the Holy Ghost by the mouth of David spake before concerning Judas, which was guide to them that took Jesus.

Acts 1:16

For had ye believed Moses, ye would have believed me: for he wrote of me. But if ye believe not his writings, how shall ye believe my words?

John 5:46,47

Jesus answered and said unto them, Ye do err, not knowing the scriptures, nor the power of God.

Matthew 22:29

For I delivered unto you first of all that which I also received, how that Christ died for our sins according to the scriptures.

I Corinthians 15:3

As newborn babes, desire the sincere milk of the word, that ye may grow thereby.

I Peter 2:2

Additional Scripture References

Deut. 17:18,19; Josh. 1:8; Ps. 119: 11; 119:105; Prov. 30:5; Jer. 15:16; 36:2; Ezek 2:9,10; Hab. 2:2; Matt. 26:56; Luke 4:21; John 2:22; 5:39; Acts 17:11; Rom. 2:1-5; Eph. 6:17; Rev. 1:1-3; 22:18,19

Blood of Christ

But God commendeth his love toward us, in that, while we were yet sinners, Christ died for us. Much more then, being now justified by his blood, we shall be saved from wrath through him.

Romans 5:8,9

To the praise of the glory of his grace, wherein he hath made us accepted in the beloved. In whom we have redemption through his blood, the forgiveness of sins, according to the riches of his grace.

Ephesians 1:6,7

And they sung a new song, saying, Thou art worthy to take the book, and to open the seals thereof: for thou wast slain, and hast redeemed us to God by thy blood out of every kindred, and tongue, and people, and nation.

Revelation 5:9

For it pleased the Father that in him should all fulness dwell; And, having made peace through the blood of his cross, by him to reconcile all things unto himself; by him, I say, whether they be things in earth, or things in heaven.

Colossians 1:19,20

And he took the cup, and gave thanks, and gave it to them, saying, Drink ye all of it;

For this is my blood of the new testament, which is shed for many for the remission of sins.

Matthew 26:27,28

Forasmuch as ye know that ye were not redeemed with corruptible things, as silver and gold, from your vain conversation received by tradition from your fathers; But with the precious blood of Christ, as of a lamb without blemish and without spot.

I Peter 1:18,19

And almost all things are by the law purged with blood; and without shedding of blood is no remission.

Hebrews 9:22

Wherefore Jesus also, that he might sanctify the people with his own blood, suffered without the gate.

Hebrews 13:12

Additional Scripture References

John 6:53-56; 19:34; Acts 20:28; Rom. 3:23-25; Eph. 2:13; Col. 1:14; 1:21,22; Heb. 9:11-28; I Jn. 1:7; 5:6-8; Rev. 1:5; 7:13-17; 12:10,11

Brotherly Love

Seeing ye have purified your souls in obeying the truth through the Spirit unto unfeigned love of the brethren, see that ye love one another with a pure heart fervently.

I Peter 1:22

But as touching brotherly love ye need not that I write unto you: for ye yourselves are taught of God to love one another.

I Thessalonians 4:9

If a man say, I love God, and hateth his brother, he is a liar: for he that loveth not his brother whom he hath seen, how can he love God whom he hath not seen? And this commandment have we from him, That he who loveth God love his brother also.

I John 4:20,21

We know that we have passed from death unto life, because we love the brethren. He that loveth not his brother abideth in death.

I John 3:14

Hereby perceive we the love of God, because he laid down his life for us: and we ought to lay down our lives for the brethren.

I John 3:16

Thou shalt not avenge, nor bear any grudge against the children of thy people, but thou shalt love thy neighbour as thyself: I am the Lord.

Leviticus 19:18

Owe no man any thing, but to love one another: for he that loveth another hath fulfilled the law.

Romans 13:8

It is good neither to eat flesh, nor to drink wine, nor any thing whereby thy brother stumbleth, or is offended, or is made weak.

Romans 14:21

But whoso hath this world's good, and seeth his brother have need, and shutteth up his bowels of compassion from him, how dwelleth the love of God in him?

I John 3:17

Take heed to yourselves: If thy brother trespass against thee, rebuke him; and if he repent, forgive him. And if he trespass against thee seven times in a day, and seven times in a day turn again to thee, saying, I repent; thou shalt forgive him.

Luke 17:3,4

Additional Scripture References

Ruth 1:16; Prov. 17:17; 18:24; Matt. 5:22-24; 22:35-40; Rom. 12:10; 14:10; I Cor. 6:1-8; 8:9-13; Gal. 5:14; I Thes. 3:12; 4:6; Heb. 13:1; I Pet. 2:17; II Pet. 1:4-15

Children of God

After this manner therefore pray ye: Our Father which art in heaven, Hallowed be thy name.

Matthew 6:9

The Spirit itself beareth witness with our spirit, that we are the children of God: And if children, then heirs; heirs of God, and joint-heirs with Christ; if so be that we suffer with him, that we may be also glorified together.

Romans 8:16,17

For ye are all the children of God by faith in Christ Jesus.

Galatians 3:26

Blessed are the peacemakers: for they shall be called the children of God.

Matthew 5:9

Now we, brethren, as Isaac was, are the children of promise.

Galatians 4:28

Neither can they die any more: for they are equal unto the angels; and are the children of God, being the children of the resurrection.

Luke 20:36

But love ye your enemies, and do good, and lend, hoping for nothing again; and your reward shall be great, and ye shall be the children of the Highest: for he is kind unto the unthankful and to the evil.

Luke 6:35

Whosoever is born of God doth not commit sin; for his seed remaineth in him: and he cannot sin, because he is born of God. In this the children of God are manifest, and the children of the devil: whosoever doeth not righteousness is not of God, neither he that loveth not his brother.

I John 3:9,10

By this we know that we love the children of God, when we love God, and keep his commandments.

I John 5:2

Ye are all the children of light, and the children of the day: we are not of the night, nor of darkness.

I Thessalonians 5:5

Additional Scripture References

Is. 8:18; Matt. 5:44-48; 13:38; John 12:36; Rom. 9:8; 9:26; Eph. 2:3; 5:8; Heb. 2:13

Christ's Return

... I go to prepare a place for you. And if I go and prepare a place for you, I will come again, and receive you unto myself; that where I am, there ye may be also.

John 14:2,3

And when he had spoken these things, while they beheld, he was taken up; and a cloud received him out of their sight. And while they looked stedfastly toward heaven as he went up, behold, two men stood by them in white apparel; Which also said, Ye men of Galilee, why stand ye gazing up into heaven? this same Jesus, which is taken up from you into heaven, shall so come in like manner as ye have seen him go into heaven.

Acts 1:9-11

For the grace of God that bringeth salvation hath appeared to all men, Teaching us that, denying ungodliness and worldly lusts, we should live soberly, righteously, and godly, in this present world; Looking for that blessed hope, and the glorious appearing of the great God and our Saviour Jesus Christ.

Titus 2:11-13

When the Son of man shall come in his glory, and all the holy angels with him, then shall he sit upon the throne of his glory.

Matthew 25:31

For the Son of man shall come in the glory of his Father with his angels; and then he shall reward every man according to his works.

Matthew 16:27

And now, little children, abide in him; that, when he shall appear, we may have confidence, and not be ashamed before him at his coming.

I John 2:28

Not forsaking the assembling of ourselves together, as the manner of some is; but exhorting one another: and so much the more, as ye see the day approaching.

Hebrews 10:25

That the trial of your faith, being much more precious than of gold that perisheth, though it be tried with fire, might be found unto praise and honour and glory at the appearing of Jesus Christ.

I Peter 1:7

Additional Scripture References

Dan. 7:13,14; Zech. 14:5; Matt. 24:3-44; 26:64; Mark 8:38; Acts 3:19-21; I Cor. 1:7; 4:5; Phil. 4:5; Col. 3:4; I Thes. 3:13; II Thes. 1:7-10; II Tim. 4:8; Heb. 9:27,28; James 5:7-9; I Pet. 1:13; 5:4; II Pet. 3:3-12; I Jn. 3:2; Jude 14; Rev. 1:7; 3:11; 19:11-16

The Church

And I say also unto thee, That thou art Peter, and upon this rock I will build my church; and the gates of hell shall not prevail against it.

Matthew 16:18

And other sheep I have, which are not of this fold: them also I must bring, and they shall hear my voice; and there shall be one fold, and one shepherd.

John 10:16

Praise ye the Lord. Sing unto the Lord a new song, and his praise in the congregation of saints.

Psalm 149:1

And hath put all things under his feet, and gave him to be the head over all things to the church, Which is his body, the fulness of him that filleth all in all.

Ephesians 1:22,23

Praising God, and having favour with all the people. And the Lord added to the church daily such as should be saved.

Acts 2:47

Take heed therefore unto yourselves, and to all the flock, over the which the Holy Ghost hath made you overseers, to feed the church of God, which he hath purchased with his own blood.

Acts 20:28

And when they had prayed, the place was shaken where they were assembled together; and they were all filled with the Holy Ghost, and they spake the word of God with boldness. And the multitude of them that believed were of one heart and of one soul.

Acts 4:31,32

And he is the head of the body, the church: who is the beginning, the firstborn from the dead; that in all things he might have the preeminence.

Colossians 1:18

For this cause I bow my knees unto the Father of our Lord Jesus Christ, Of whom the whole family in heaven and earth is named.

Ephesians 3:14,15

For as we have many members in one body, and all members have not the same office: So we, being many, are one body in Christ, and every one members one of another.

Romans 12:4,5

Additional Scripture References

Acts 1:15; 5:42; I Cor. 1:2; 3:9; 10:17; 10:31,32; 12:27,28; 15:9; II Cor. 11:2; Eph. 2:19-22; 5:23-33; Col. 1:24; I Tim. 3:15; Heb. 12:22-24; I Pet. 5:2

No Condemnation
for the Believer in Christ

He that believeth on him is not condemned: but he that believeth not is condemned already, because he hath not believed in the name of the only begotten Son of God.

John 3:18

Verily, verily, I say unto you, He that heareth my word, and believeth on him that sent me, hath everlasting life, and shall not come into condemnation; but is passed from death unto life.

John 5:24

Blessed is the man to whom the Lord will not impute sin.

Romans 4:8

Therefore being justified by faith, we have peace with God through our Lord Jesus Christ.

Romans 5:1

There is therefore now no condemnation to them which are in Christ Jesus, who walk not after the flesh, but after the Spirit.

Romans 8:1

For if the ministration of condemnation be glory, much more doth the ministration of righteousness exceed in glory.

II Corinthians 3:9

No weapon that is formed against thee shall prosper; and every tongue that shall rise against thee in judgment thou shalt condemn. This is the heritage of the servants of the Lord, and their righteousness is of me, saith the Lord.

Isaiah 54:17

For God hath not appointed us to wrath, but to obtain salvation by our Lord Jesus Christ.

I Thessalonians 5:9

But we are bound to give thanks alway to God for you, brethren beloved of the Lord, because God hath from the beginning chosen you to salvation through sanctification of the Spirit and belief of the truth: Whereunto he called you by our gospel, to the obtaining of the glory of our Lord Jesus Christ.

II Thessalonians 2:13,14

Who are kept by the power of God through faith unto salvation ready to be revealed in the last time.

I Peter 1:5

Additional Scripture References

Ps. 32:2; Is. 50:9; 53:9-12; Rom. 8:34; II Cor. 5:19-21; Gal. 3:13; I Jn. 3:21; 5:12

Confessing Christ

That if thou shalt confess with thy mouth the Lord Jesus, and shalt believe in thine heart that God hath raised him from the dead, thou shalt be saved.

Romans 10:9

Whosoever shall confess that Jesus is the Son of God, God dwelleth in him, and he in God.

I John 4:15

Whosoever therefore shall confess me before men, him will I confess also before my Father which is in heaven.

Matthew 10:32

Hereby know ye the Spirit of God: Every spirit that confesseth that Jesus Christ is come in the flesh is of God.

I John 4:2

Also I say unto you, Whosoever shall confess me before men, him shall the Son of man also confess before the angels of God.

Luke 12:8

That at the name of Jesus every knee should bow, of things in heaven, and things in earth, and things under the earth; And that every tongue should confess that Jesus Christ is Lord, to the glory of God the Father.

Philippians 2:10,11

Whosoever denieth the Son, the same hath not the Father: [but] he that acknowledgeth the Son hath the Father also.

I John 2:23

Wherefore I give you to understand, that no man speaking by the Spirit of God calleth Jesus accursed: and that no man can say that Jesus is the Lord, but by the Holy Ghost.

I Corinthians 12:3

For many deceivers are entered into the world, who confess not that Jesus Christ is come in the flesh. This is a deceiver and an antichrist.

II John 7

But when the Comforter is come, whom I will send unto you from the Father, even the Spirit of truth, which proceedeth from the Father, he shall testify of me.

John 15:26

Additional Scripture References

Mark 8:38; Luke 6:46; John 12:42,43; 13:13; Acts 2:36; 8:27-39; Rom. 10:11; II Tim. 2:12; II Jn. 9

Confession of Sins

If we confess our sins, he is faithful and just to forgive us our sins, and to cleanse us from all unrighteousness.

I John 1:9

And I prayed unto the Lord my God, and made my confession, and said, O Lord, the great and dreadful God, keeping the covenant and mercy to them that love him, and to them that keep his commandments; We have sinned, and have committed iniquity, and have done wickedly, and have rebelled, even by departing from thy precepts and from thy judgments.

Daniel 9:4,5

He that covereth his sins shall not prosper: but whoso confesseth and forsaketh them shall have mercy.

Proverbs 28:13

I acknowledged my sin unto thee, and mine iniquity have I not hid. I said, I will confess my transgressions unto the Lord; and thou forgavest the iniquity of my sin. Selah.

Psalm 32:5

For I will declare mine iniquity; I will be sorry for my sin.

Psalm 38:18

And Hezekiah spake comfortably unto all the Levites that taught the good knowledge of the Lord: and they did eat throughout the feast seven days, offering peace offerings, and making confession to the Lord God of their fathers.

II Chronicles 30:22

And David said unto Nathan, I have sinned against the Lord. And Nathan said unto David, The Lord also hath put away thy sin; thou shalt not die.

II Samuel 12:13

Then went out to him Jerusalem, and all Judaea, and all the region round about Jordan, And were baptized of him in Jordan, confessing their sins.

Matthew 3:5,6

For it is written, As I live, saith the Lord, every knee shall bow to me, and every tongue shall confess to God.

Romans 14:11

How many are mine iniquities and sins? make me to know my transgression and my sin.

Job 13:23

Additional Scripture References

Lev. 26:40-42; Jud. 10:10; I Sam. 7:6; I Kin. 8:30-36; II Chr. 6:24-27; Ps. 51:2-4; 66:18-20; Is. 59:12; Dan. 9:20-23

Courage

Be of good courage, and he shall strengthen your heart, all ye that hope in the Lord.

Psalm 31:24

For God hath not given us the spirit of fear; but of power, and of love, and of a sound mind.

II Timothy 1:7

For he shall give his angels charge over thee, to keep thee in all thy ways. They shall bear thee up in their hands, lest thou dash thy foot against a stone.

Psalm 91:11,12

Fear thou not; for I am with thee: be not dismayed; for I am thy God: I will strengthen thee; yea, I will help thee; yea, I will uphold thee with the right hand of my righteousness.

Isaiah 41:10

Be strong and courageous, be not afraid nor dismayed for the king of Assyria, nor for all the multitude that is with him: for there be more with us than with him: With him is an arm of flesh; but with us is the Lord our God to help us, and to fight our battles. And the people rested themselves upon the words of Hezekiah king of Judah.

II Chronicles 32:7,8

Have not I commanded thee? Be strong and of a good courage; be not afraid, neither be thou dismayed: for the Lord thy God is with thee whithersoever thou goest.

Joshua 1:9

Watch ye, stand fast in the faith, quit you like men, be strong.

I Corinthians 16:13

Hearken unto me, ye that know righteousness, the people in whose heart is my law; fear ye not the reproach of men, neither be ye afraid of their revilings.

Isaiah 51:7

Be not afraid of their faces: for I am with thee to deliver thee, saith the Lord.

Jeremiah 1:8

Then shalt thou prosper, if thou takest heed to fulfil the statutes and judgments which the Lord charged Moses with concerning Israel: be strong, and of good courage; dread not, nor be dismayed.

I Chronicles 22:13

Additional Scripture References

Lev. 26:6-8; Deut. 31:7,8; Josh. 1:1-9; 23:6; I Chr. 19:13; Is. 51:12-16; Phil. 1:27,28

Covetousness - Greed

Thou shalt not covet thy neighbour's house, thou shalt not covet thy neighbour's wife, nor his manservant, nor his maidservant, nor his ox, nor his ass, nor any thing that is thy neighbour's.

Exodus 20:17

And he said unto them, Take heed, and beware of covetousness: for a man's life consisteth not in the abundance of the things which he possesseth.

Luke 12:15

The prince that wanteth understanding is also a great oppressor: but he that hateth covetousness shall prolong his days.

Proverbs 28:16

For we brought nothing into this world, and it is certain we can carry nothing out.

I Timothy 6:7

For the love of money is the root of all evil: which while some coveted after, they have erred from the faith, and pierced themselves through with many sorrows.

I Timothy 6:10

As the partridge sitteth on eggs, and hatcheth them not; so he that getteth riches, and not by right, shall leave them in the midst of his days, and at his end shall be a fool.

Jeremiah 17:11

Set your affection on things above, not on things on the earth.

Colossians 3:2

Mortify therefore your members which are upon the earth; fornication, uncleanness, inordinate affection, evil concupiscence, and covetousness, which is idolatry: For which things' sake the wrath of God cometh on the children of disobedience.

Colossians 3:5,6

Hell and destruction are never full; so the eyes of man are never satisfied.

Proverbs 27:20

But fornication, and all uncleanness, or covetousness, let it not be once named among you, as becometh saints.

Ephesians 5:3

Additional Scripture References

Ps. 119:36; Prov. 1:15-19; 11:24; 15:27; 21:25,26; 23:1-8; Ecc. 5:10,11; Is. 56:11; 57:17; Mark 7:21-23; Rom. 1:28-32; I Cor. 5:9-13; 6:9,10; II Cor. 9:5; Eph. 5:5; I Thes. 2:5; I Tim. 3:1-3; 3:8; II Tim. 3:1-7; Heb. 13:5

Death

But I would not have you to be ignorant, brethren, concerning them which are asleep, that ye sorrow not, even as others which have no hope. For if we believe that Jesus died and rose again, even so them also which sleep in Jesus will God bring with him. For this we say unto you by the word of the Lord, that we which are alive and remain unto the coming of the Lord shall not prevent them which are asleep. For the Lord himself shall descend from heaven with a shout, with the voice of the archangel, and with the trump of God: and the dead in Christ shall rise first: Then we which are alive and remain shall be caught up together with them in the clouds, to meet the Lord in the air: and so shall we ever be with the Lord.

I Thessalonians 4:13-17

But of the tree of the knowledge of good and evil, thou shalt not eat of it: for in the day that thou eatest thereof thou shalt surely die.

Genesis 2:17

He will swallow up death in victory; and the Lord God will wipe away tears from off all faces; and the rebuke of his people shall he take away from off all the earth: for the Lord hath spoken it.

Isaiah 25:8

Verily, verily, I say unto you, He that heareth my word, and believeth on him that sent me, hath everlasting life, and shall not come into condemnation; but is passed from death unto life.

John 5:24

So when this corruptible shall have put on incorruption, and this mortal shall have put on immortality, then shall be brought to pass the saying that is written, Death is swallowed up in victory. O death, where is thy sting? O grave, where is thy victory?

I Corinthians 15:54,55

For to me to live is Christ, and to die is gain.

Philippians 1:21

Additional Scripture References

II Chr. 15:12-15; Ps. 56:13; 116:15; Prov. 10:2; 12:28; 14:12; John 8:51; Rom. 5:12-21; 6:23; 8:2; 8:6; 8:13; 8:38,39; I Cor. 15:26; II Tim. 1:10; Heb. 2:14,15; 9:27; I Jn. 3:14; Rev. 20:14; 21:4

Deliverance

Because he hath set his love upon me, therefore will I deliver him: I will set him on high, because he hath known my name. He shall call upon me, and I will answer him: I will be with him in trouble; I will deliver him, and honour him.

Psalm 91:14,15

Who hath delivered us from the power of darkness, and hath translated us into the kingdom of his dear Son.

Colossians 1:13

The righteous cry, and the Lord heareth, and delivereth them out of all their troubles.

Psalm 34:17

Offer unto God thanksgiving; and pay thy vows unto the most High: And call upon me in the day of trouble: I will deliver thee, and thou shalt glorify me.

Psalm 50:14,15

Because the creature itself also shall be delivered from the bondage of corruption into the glorious liberty of the children of God.

Romans 8:21

The Lord knoweth how to deliver the godly out of temptations, and to reserve the unjust unto the day of judgment to be punished.

II Peter 2:9

And the Lord shall deliver me from every evil work, and will preserve me unto his heavenly kingdom: to whom be glory for ever and ever. Amen.

II Timothy 4:18

Who gave himself for our sins, that he might deliver us from this present evil world, according to the will of God and our Father.

Galatians 1:4

Blessed is he that considereth the poor: the Lord will deliver him in time of trouble.

Psalm 41:1

He that trusteth in his own heart is a fool: but whoso walketh wisely, he shall be delivered.

Proverbs 28:26

Additional Scripture References

I Sam. 7:3; 17:37; Job 5:19;
Ps. 18:1-20; 22:4; 34:19; 37:39,40; 72:12;
Prov. 11:9; 11:21; Dan. 3:29; 6:26,27;
II Cor. 1:10; I Thes. 1:10

Discipleship

And he saith unto them, Follow me, and I will make you fishers of men.

Matthew 4:19

And the things that thou hast heard of me among many witnesses, the same commit thou to faithful men, who shall be able to teach others also.

II Timothy 2:2

Study to shew thyself approved unto God, a workman that needeth not to be ashamed, rightly dividing the word of truth.

II Timothy 2:15

A new commandment I give unto you, That ye love one another; as I have loved you, that ye also love one another. By this shall all men know that ye are my disciples, if ye have love one to another.

John 13:34,35

Go ye therefore, and teach all nations, baptizing them in the name of the Father, and of the Son, and of the Holy Ghost: Teaching them to observe all things whatsoever I have commanded you: and, lo, I am with you alway, even unto the end of the world. Amen.

Matthew 28:19,20

Then said Jesus to them again, Peace be unto you: as my Father hath sent me, even so send I you.

John 20:21

Brethren, be followers together of me, and mark them which walk so as ye have us for an ensample.

Philippians 3:17

Herein is my Father glorified, that ye bear much fruit; so shall ye be my disciples.

John 15:8

As every man hath received the gift, even so minister the same one to another, as good stewards of the manifold grace of God.

I Peter 4:10

So likewise, whosoever he be of you that forsaketh not all that he hath, he cannot be my disciple.

Luke 14:33

Then said Jesus to those Jews which believed on him, If ye continue in my word, then are ye my disciples indeed.

John 8:31

Additional Scripture References

Matt. 9:35-38; Luke 14:25-33; I Cor. 9:19-23; 11:1; II Cor. 3:6; Phil. 4:9; I Thes. 2:1-20; II Tim. 2:15-26; 4:2

Doubt

I will therefore that men pray every where, lifting up holy hands, without wrath and doubting.

I Timothy 2:8

But let him ask in faith, nothing wavering. For he that wavereth is like a wave of the sea driven with the wind and tossed. For let not that man think that he shall receive any thing of the Lord. A double minded man is unstable in all his ways.

James 1:6-8

If thou faint in the day of adversity, thy strength is small.

Proverbs 24:10

Jesus said unto him, If thou canst believe, all things are possible to him that believeth.

Mark 9:23

Jesus answered and said unto them, Verily I say unto you, If ye have faith, and doubt not, ye shall not only do this which is done to the fig tree, but also if ye shall say unto this mountain, Be thou removed, and be thou cast into the sea; it shall be done. And all things, whatsoever ye shall ask in prayer, believing, ye shall receive.

Matthew 21:21,22

Jesus saith unto him, Thomas, because thou hast seen me, thou hast believed: blessed are they that have not seen, and yet have believed.

John 20:29

And he saith unto them, Why are ye fearful, O ye of little faith? Then he arose, and rebuked the winds and the sea; and there was a great calm.

Matthew 8:26

Therefore I say unto you, What things soever ye desire, when ye pray, believe that ye receive them, and ye shall have them.

Mark 11:24

And seek not ye what ye shall eat, or what ye shall drink, neither be ye of doubtful mind.

Luke 12:29

While Peter thought on the vision, the Spirit said unto him, Behold, three men seek thee. Arise therefore, and get thee down, and go with them, doubting nothing: for I have sent them.

Acts 10:19,20

Additional Scripture References

Matt. 11:2-6; 14:22-31; 17:14-21

Envy - Jealousy

A sound heart is the life of the flesh: but envy the rottenness of the bones.

Proverbs 14:30

For where envying and strife is, there is confusion and every evil work.

James 3:16

For jealousy is the rage of a man: therefore he will not spare in the day of vengeance.

Proverbs 6:34

Charity suffereth long, and is kind; charity envieth not; charity vaunteth not itself, is not puffed up.

I Corinthians 13:4

Set me as a seal upon thine heart, as a seal upon thine arm: for love is strong as death; jealousy is cruel as the grave: the coals thereof are coals of fire, which hath a most vehement flame.

Song of Solomon 8:6

Let us not be desirous of vain glory, provoking one another, envying one another.

Galatians 5:26

Grudge not one against another, brethren, lest ye be condemned: behold, the judge standeth before the door.

James 5:9

Wherefore laying aside all malice, and all guile, and hypocrisies, and envies, and all evil speakings.

I Peter 2:1

Let us walk honestly, as in the day; not in rioting and drunkenness, not in chambering and wantonness, not in strife and envying.

Romans 13:13

For wrath killeth the foolish man, and envy slayeth the silly one.

Job 5:2

Additional Scripture References

Ps. 37:7; 49:16; Prov. 3:31; 24:1; 24:19; 27:4; Rom. 1:28-32, I Cor. 3:3; Gal. 5:19-26; Titus 3:3

Eternal Life

For God so loved the world, that he gave his only begotten Son, that whosoever believeth in him should not perish, but have everlasting life.

John 3:16

For the wages of sin is death; but the gift of God is eternal life through Jesus Christ our Lord.

Romans 6:23

Be not deceived; God is not mocked: for whatsoever a man soweth, that shall he also reap. For he that soweth to his flesh shall of the flesh reap corruption; but he that soweth to the Spirit shall of the Spirit reap life everlasting.

Galatians 6:7,8

He that believeth on the Son hath everlasting life: and he that believeth not the Son shall not see life; but the wrath of God abideth on him.

John 3:36

In hope of eternal life, which God, that cannot lie, promised before the world began.

Titus 1:2

But thou, O man of God, flee these things; and follow after righteousness, godliness, faith, love, patience, meekness. Fight the good fight of faith, lay hold on eternal life, whereunto thou art also called, and hast pro-

fessed a good profession before many witnesses.

I Timothy 6:11,12

That as sin hath reigned unto death,
even so might grace reign through righteousness unto eternal life by Jesus Christ our Lord.

Romans 5:21

But whosoever drinketh of the water
that I shall give him shall never thirst; but the
water that I shall give him shall be in him a well
of water springing up into everlasting life.

John 4:14

Labour not for the meat which perisheth, but for that meat which endureth unto
everlasting life, which the Son of man shall give
unto you: for him hath God the Father sealed.

John 6:27

Additional Scripture References

*Ps. 21:4; 121:8; Dan. 12:2; Mark 10:29,30;
Luke 10:25-37; 20:36; John 4:34-36; 6:40;
6:47; 6:53,54; 6:58; 10:10; 10:27,28; 12:25;
17:1-3; Acts 13:48; Rom. 2:6,7;
I Cor. 15:53-55; II Cor. 4:17; 5:1-4; Heb. 5:9;
I Pet. 1:3,4; I John 2:25; 5:11-13*

Faith

Now faith is the substance of things hoped for, the evidence of things not seen.

Hebrews 11:1

So then faith cometh by hearing, and hearing by the word of God.

Romans 10:17

Wherefore the law was our schoolmaster to bring us unto Christ, that we might be justified by faith. But after that faith is come, we are no longer under a schoolmaster. For ye are all the children of God by faith in Christ Jesus.

Galatians 3:24-26

For by grace are ye saved through faith; and that not of yourselves: it is the gift of God: Not of works, lest any man should boast.

Ephesians 2:8,9

For whatsoever is born of God overcometh the world: and this is the victory that overcometh the world, even our faith.

I John 5:4

Jesus said unto him, If thou canst believe, all things are possible to him that believeth.

Mark 9:23

Therefore being justified by faith, we have peace with God through our Lord Jesus Christ: By whom also we have access by faith into this grace wherein we stand, and rejoice in hope of the glory of God.

Romans 5:1,2

Above all, taking the shield of faith, wherewith ye shall be able to quench all the fiery darts of the wicked.

Ephesians 6:16

Being justified freely by his grace through the redemption that is in Christ Jesus: Whom God hath set forth to be a propitiation through faith in his blood, to declare his righteousness for the remission of sins that are past, through the forbearance of God.

Romans 3:24,25

(For we walk by faith, not by sight.)

II Corinthians 5:7

Additional Scripture References

Matt. 6:25-34; 9:22; 9:29; 21:21,22; Luke 17:6; John 11:40; Rom. 3:28; 4:5; 10:8-11; I Cor. 2:5; Gal. 3:1-29; Eph. 3:14-19; Phil. 3:7-11; Col. 1:21-23; II Thes. 2:13; I Tim. 1:1-5; 6:11,12; Heb. 10:38,39; 11:1-40

Fear

Fear thou not; for I am with thee: be not dismayed; for I am thy God: I will strengthen thee; yea, I will help thee; yea, I will uphold thee with the right hand of my righteousness.

Isaiah 41:10

For God hath not given us the spirit of fear; but of power, and of love, and of a sound mind.

II Timothy 1:7

Be careful for nothing; but in every thing by prayer and supplication with thanksgiving let your requests be made known unto God. And the peace of God, which passeth all understanding, shall keep your hearts and minds through Christ Jesus.

Philippians 4:6,7

Have not I commanded thee? Be strong and of a good courage; be not afraid, neither be thou dismayed: for the Lord thy God is with thee whithersoever thou goest.

Joshua 1:9

Peace I leave with you, my peace I give unto you: not as the world giveth, give I unto you. Let not your heart be troubled, neither let it be afraid.

John 14:27

The Lord is my light and my salvation; whom shall I fear? the Lord is the strength of my life; of whom shall I be afraid?

Psalm 27:1

What time I am afraid, I will trust in thee. In God I will praise his word, in God I have put my trust; I will not fear what flesh can do unto me.

Psalm 56:3,4

No weapon that is formed against thee shall prosper; and every tongue that shall rise against thee in judgment thou shalt condemn. This is the heritage of the servants of the Lord, and their righteousness is of me, saith the Lord.

Isaiah 54:17

So that we may boldly say, The Lord is my helper, and I will not fear what man shall do unto me.

Hebrews 13:6

. . . Be not afraid, only believe.

Mark 5:36

Additional Scripture References

Gen. 15:1; Num. 14:8,9; Ps. 23:4; 91:1-16; 112:1-10; 118:6; Prov. 1:27-33; 3:25,26; Is. 35:4; 51:7-16; Dan. 10:1-21; Matt. 10:28; Rom. 8:15; I Pet. 3:12-16; I Jn. 4:18

Fear of God

Behold, the eye of the Lord is upon them that fear him, upon them that hope in his mercy.

Psalm 33:18

The fear of the Lord is the beginning of wisdom: and the knowledge of the holy is understanding.

Proverbs 9:10

By mercy and truth iniquity is purged: and by the fear of the Lord men depart from evil.

Proverbs 16:6

Then they that feared the Lord spake often one to another: and the Lord hearkened, and heard it, and a book of remembrance was written before him for them that feared the Lord, and that thought upon his name.

Malachi 3:16

Only fear the Lord, and serve him in truth with all your heart: for consider how great things he hath done for you.

I Samuel 12:24

But the mercy of the Lord is from everlasting to everlasting upon them that fear him, and his righteousness unto children's children.

Psalm 103:17

Who shall not fear thee, O Lord, and glorify thy name? for thou only art holy: for all nations shall come and worship before thee; for thy judgments are made manifest.

Revelation 15:4

O that there were such an heart in them, that they would fear me, and keep all my commandments always, that it might be well with them, and with their children for ever!

Deuteronomy 5:29

Teach me thy way, O Lord; I will walk in thy truth: unite my heart to fear thy name.

Psalm 86:11

Let us hear the conclusion of the whole matter: Fear God, and keep his commandments: for this is the whole duty of man.

Ecclesiastes 12:13

Additional Scripture References

Ex. 18:21; I Sam. 12:14,15; I Chr. 16:25-27; Ps. 19:7-11; 25:12-14; 31:19,20; 145:19; Prov. 10:27; 14:26,27; 15:16; 19:23; 31:30; Jer. 5:21-25; Luke 1:50; II Cor. 7:1; Heb. 12:28; I Pet. 2:17; Rev. 14:6,7

Fellowship - Unity

But if we walk in the light, as he is in the light, we have fellowship one with another, and the blood of Jesus Christ his Son cleanseth us from all sin.

I John 1:7

Behold, how good and how pleasant it is for brethren to dwell together in unity!

Psalm 133:1

And we beseech you, brethren, to know them which labour among you, and are over you in the Lord, and admonish you; And to esteem them very highly in love for their work's sake. And be at peace among yourselves.

I Thessalonians 5:12,13

That which we have seen and heard declare we unto you, that ye also may have fellowship with us: and truly our fellowship is with the Father, and with his Son Jesus Christ.

I John 1:3

Two are better than one; because they have a good reward for their labour. For if they fall, the one will lift up his fellow: but woe to him that is alone when he falleth; for he hath not another to help him up.

Ecclesiastes 4:9,10

Now the God of patience and consolation grant you to be likeminded one toward another according to Christ Jesus: That ye may with one mind and one mouth glorify God, even the Father of our Lord Jesus Christ.

Romans 15:5,6

Bear ye one another's burdens, and so fulfil the law of Christ.

Galatians 6:2

For where two or three are gathered together in my name, there am I in the midst of them.

Matthew 18:20

I therefore, the prisoner of the Lord, beseech you that ye walk worthy of the vocation wherewith ye are called, With all lowliness and meekness, with longsuffering, forbearing one another in love; Endeavouring to keep the unity of the Spirit in the bond of peace.

Ephesians 4:1-3

As we have therefore opportunity, let us do good unto all men, especially unto them who are of the household of faith.

Galatians 6:10

Additional Scripture References

Lev. 26:12; Ps. 55:14; Is. 57:15; Acts 2:42; 2:44-47; Rom. 1:12; 12:16; I Cor. 1:9,10; 10:16; 12:12-14; II Cor. 13:11; Eph. 2:13-22; 4:11-13; 4:32; Phil. 1:3-5; Col. 3:16; Heb. 10:24,25; I Pet. 3:8,9

Finances

But seek ye first the kingdom of God, and his righteousness; and all these things shall be added unto you.

Matthew 6:33

Bring ye all the tithes into the storehouse, that there may be meat in mine house, and prove me now herewith, saith the Lord of hosts, if I will not open you the windows of heaven, and pour you out a blessing, that there shall not be room enough to receive it.

Malachi 3:10

Let not mercy and truth forsake thee: bind them about thy neck; write them upon the table of thine heart: So shalt thou find favour and good understanding in the sight of God and man.

Proverbs 3:3,4

And God is able to make all grace abound toward you; that ye, always having all sufficiency in all things, may abound to every good work.

II Corinthians 9:8

The silver is mine, and the gold is mine, saith the Lord of hosts.

Haggai 2:8

He that hasteth to be rich hath an evil eye, and considereth not that poverty shall come upon him.

Proverbs 28:22

He becometh poor that dealeth with a slack hand: but the hand of the diligent maketh rich.

Proverbs 10:4

Honour the Lord with thy substance, and with the firstfruits of all thine increase: So shall thy barns be filled with plenty, and thy presses shall burst out with new wine.

Proverbs 3:9,10

For which of you, intending to build a tower, sitteth not down first, and counteth the cost, whether he have sufficient to finish it?

Luke 14:28

And having food and raiment let us be therewith content.

I Timothy 6:8

Additional Scripture References

Deut. 8:18; 10:14; Ps. 24:1; 37:21; 84:11; 112:1-3; Prov. 6:6-11; 12:24; 13:11; 15:16; 19:17; 22:4; Matt. 6:19-21; Luke 6:38; 16:10-12; Acts 20:35; Rom. 8:32; II Cor. 9:6; Gal. 3:18,29; Phil. 4:15-19; I Tim. 6:17; III Jn. 2

Forgiveness of Sins

If we confess our sins, he is faithful and just to forgive us our sins, and to cleanse us from all unrighteousness.

I John 1:9

In whom we have redemption through his blood, the forgiveness of sins, according to the riches of his grace.

Ephesians 1:7

As far as the east is from the west, so far hath he removed our transgressions from us.

Psalm 103:12

For this is my blood of the new testament, which is shed for many for the remission of sins.

Matthew 26:28

If my people, which are called by my name, shall humble themselves, and pray, and seek my face, and turn from their wicked ways; then will I hear from heaven, and will forgive their sin, and will heal their land.

II Chronicles 7:14

And you, being dead in your sins and the uncircumcision of your flesh, hath he quickened together with him, having forgiven you all trespasses.

Colossians 2:13

I acknowledged my sin unto thee, and mine iniquity have I not hid. I said, I will confess my transgressions unto the Lord; and thou forgavest the iniquity of my sin. Selah.

Psalm 32:5

For thou, Lord, art good, and ready to forgive; and plenteous in mercy unto all them that call upon thee.

Psalm 86:5

And almost all things are by the law purged with blood; and without shedding of blood is no remission.

Hebrews 9:22

But that ye may know that the Son of man hath power on earth to forgive sins.

Matthew 9:6

Come now, and let us reason together, saith the Lord: though your sins be as scarlet, they shall be as white as snow; though they be red like crimson, they shall be as wool.

Isaiah 1:18

Additional Scripture References

Num. 14:17-21; 15:15-28; I Kin. 8:36;
Ps. 130:3,4; Is. 55:7; Jer. 31:33,34;
Matt. 5:23,24; 6:14,15; 12:31,32; 18:21-35;
Luke 1:76,77; 17:3,4; Acts 2:38; 13:38,39;
26:15-18

Forgiving Others

And be ye kind one to another, tender-hearted, forgiving one another, even as God for Christ's sake hath forgiven you.

Ephesians 4:32

And when ye stand praying, forgive, if ye have ought against any: that your Father also which is in heaven may forgive you your trespasses. But if ye do not forgive, neither will your Father which is in heaven forgive your trespasses.

Mark 11:25,26

And forgive us our debts, as we forgive our debtors... For if ye forgive men their trespasses, your heavenly Father will also forgive you: But if ye forgive not men their trespasses, neither will your Father forgive your trespasses.

Matthew 6:12,14,15

Take heed to yourselves: If thy brother trespass against thee, rebuke him; and if he repent, forgive him. And if he trespass against thee seven times in a day, and seven times in a day turn again to thee, saying, I repent; thou shalt forgive him.

Luke 17:3,4

Bless them which persecute you: bless, and curse not.

Romans 12:14

Then said Jesus, Father, forgive them; for they know not what they do.

Luke 23:34

And they stoned Stephen, calling upon God, and saying, Lord Jesus, receive my spirit. And he kneeled down, and cried with a loud voice, Lord, lay not this sin to their charge. And when he had said this, he fell asleep.

Acts 7:59,60

Say not, I will do so to him as he hath done to me: I will render to the man according to his work.

Proverbs 24:29

Finally, be ye all of one mind, having compassion one of another, love as brethren, be pitiful, be courteous: Not rendering evil for evil, or railing for railing: but contrariwise blessing; knowing that ye are thereunto called, that ye should inherit a blessing.

I Peter 3:8,9

Be not overcome of evil, but overcome evil with good.

Romans 12:21

Additional Scripture References

Ex. 23:4,5; Matt. 5:43-48; 18:21-35;
Luke 6:27-38; II Cor. 2:7; Col. 3:13

Fruit of the Spirit

But the fruit of the Spirit is love, joy, peace, longsuffering, gentleness, goodness, faith, Meekness, temperance: against such there is no law.

Galatians 5:22,23

Put on therefore, as the elect of God, holy and beloved, bowels of mercies, kindness, humbleness of mind, meekness, longsuffering; Forbearing one another, and forgiving one another, if any man have a quarrel against any: even as Christ forgave you, so also do ye. And above all these things put on charity, which is the bond of perfectness. And let the peace of God rule in your hearts, to the which also ye are called in one body; and be ye thankful.

Colossians 3:12-15

But thou, O man of God, flee these things; and follow after righteousness, godliness, faith, love, patience, meekness.

I Timothy 6:11

Grace and peace be multiplied unto you through the knowledge of God, and of Jesus our Lord, According as his divine power hath given unto us all things that pertain unto life and godliness, through the knowledge of him that hath called us to glory and virtue.

II Peter 1:2,3

And I myself also am persuaded of you, my brethren, that ye also are full of goodness, filled with all knowledge, able also to admonish one another.

Romans 15:14

(For the fruit of the Spirit is in all goodness and righteousness and truth.)

Ephesians 5:9

My brethren, count it all joy when ye fall into divers temptations; Knowing this, that the trying of your faith worketh patience. But let patience have her perfect work, that ye may be perfect and entire, wanting nothing.

James 1:2-4

And the servant of the Lord must not strive; but be gentle unto all men, apt to teach, patient, In meekness instructing those that oppose themselves; if God peradventure will give them repentance to the acknowledging of the truth.

II Timothy 2:24,25

Additional Scripture References

John 13:35; 15:1,2; 15:11; Rom. 8:5; 11:22; II Cor. 6:1-10; Gal. 5:13; 5:25; Eph. 4:1,2; Phil. 4:5; 4:7; Heb. 6:11-15; II Pet. 1:4-8

Gifts of the Spirit

But the manifestation of the Spirit is given to every man to profit withal. For to one is given by the Spirit the word of wisdom; to another the word of knowledge by the same Spirit; To another faith by the same Spirit; to another the gifts of healing by the same Spirit; To another the working of miracles; to another prophecy; to another discerning of spirits; to another divers kinds of tongues; to another the interpretation of tongues: But all these worketh that one and the selfsame Spirit, dividing to every man severally as he will.

I Corinthians 12:7-11

Wherefore I put thee in remembrance that thou stir up the gift of God, which is in thee by the putting on of my hands.

II Timothy 1:6

God also bearing them witness, both with signs and wonders, and with divers miracles, and gifts of the Holy Ghost, according to his own will?

Hebrews 2:4

As every man hath received the gift, even so minister the same one to another, as good stewards of the manifold grace of God.

I Peter 4:10

And God hath set some in the church, first apostles, secondarily prophets, thirdly teachers, after that miracles, then gifts of healings, helps, governments, diversities of tongues.

I Corinthians 12:28

Long time therefore abode they speaking boldly in the Lord, which gave testimony unto the word of his grace, and granted signs and wonders to be done by their hands.

Acts 14:3

Now there are diversities of gifts, but the same Spirit. And there are differences of administrations, but the same Lord.

I Corinthians 12:4,5

Neglect not the gift that is in thee, which was given thee by prophecy, with the laying on of the hands of the presbytery.

I Timothy 4:14

But unto every one of us is given grace according to the measure of the gift of Christ.

Ephesians 4:7

Additional Scripture References

*Joel 2:28,29; Matt. 12:28; Mark 16:20;
Acts 2:1-4; 10:44-46; 19:6; Rom. 12:5-8;
I Cor. 14:1-4*

Giving

But this I say, He which soweth sparingly shall reap also sparingly; and he which soweth bountifully shall reap also bountifully. Every man according as he purposeth in his heart, so let him give; not grudgingly, or of necessity: for God loveth a cheerful giver.

II Corinthians 9:6,7

Give, and it shall be given unto you; good measure, pressed down, and shaken together, and running over, shall men give into your bosom. For with the same measure that ye mete withal it shall be measured to you again.

Luke 6:38

And if thou draw out thy soul to the hungry, and satisfy the afflicted soul; then shall thy light rise in obscurity, and thy darkness be as the noon day.

Isaiah 58:10

Every man shall give as he is able, according to the blessing of the Lord thy God which he hath given thee.

Deuteronomy 16:17

Take heed that ye do not your alms before men, to be seen of them: otherwise ye have no reward of your Father which is in heaven.

Matthew 6:1

. . . he that giveth, let him do it with simplicity; he that ruleth, with diligence; he that sheweth mercy, with cheerfulness.

Romans 12:8

Then the disciples, every man according to his ability, determined to send relief unto the brethren which dwelt in Judaea.

Acts 11:29

But whoso hath this world's good, and seeth his brother have need, and shutteth up his bowels of compassion from him, how dwelleth the love of God in him? My little children, let us not love in word, neither in tongue; but in deed and in truth.

I John 3:17,18

I have shewed you all things, how that so labouring ye ought to support the weak, and to remember the words of the Lord Jesus, how he said, It is more blessed to give than to receive.

Acts 20:35

Additional Scripture References

Deut. 15:10; I Chr. 29:17; Ps. 41:1;
Prov. 11:24,25; 19:17; 22:9; 25:21; Ecc. 11:1;
Matt. 10:42; Luke 12:33; II Cor. 8:9-15;
Eph. 6:8

Glorifying God

Whether therefore ye eat, or drink, or whatsoever ye do, do all to the glory of God.

I Corinthians 10:31

For of him, and through him, and to him, are all things: to whom be glory for ever. Amen.

Romans 11:36

Whoso offereth praise glorifieth me: and to him that ordereth his conversation aright will I shew the salvation of God.

Psalm 50:23

If ye abide in me, and my words abide in you, ye shall ask what ye will, and it shall be done unto you. Herein is my Father glorified, that ye bear much fruit; so shall ye be my disciples.

John 15:7,8

For ye are bought with a price: therefore glorify God in your body, and in your spirit, which are God's.

I Corinthians 6:20

Let your light so shine before men, that they may see your good works, and glorify your Father which is in heaven.

Matthew 5:16

Not unto us, O Lord, not unto us, but unto thy name give glory, for thy mercy, and for thy truth's sake.

Psalm 115:1

Give unto the Lord, ye kindreds of the people, give unto the Lord glory and strength. Give unto the Lord the glory due unto his name: bring an offering, and come before him: worship the Lord in the beauty of holiness.

I Chronicles 16:28,29

I have glorified thee on the earth: I have finished the work which thou gavest me to do.

John 17:4

Additional Scripture References

I Chr. 29:10-13; Ps. 18:46; 19:1; 46:10; 50:14,15; 86:9; 99:9; Is. 2:17; 25:1; Ezek. 28:22; Hag. 1:8; Luke 5:25; 13:13; 18:43; John 13:31; Rom. 4:20; 15:6; Rev. 5:13; 11:13; 14:6,7; 15:4

Healing

Heal me, O Lord, and I shall be healed; save me, and I shall be saved: for thou art my praise.

Jeremiah 17:14

And his name through faith in his name hath made this man strong, whom ye see and know: yea, the faith which is by him hath given him this perfect soundness in the presence of you all.

Acts 3:16

Is any sick among you? let him call for the elders of the church; and let them pray over him, anointing him with oil in the name of the Lord: And the prayer of faith shall save the sick, and the Lord shall raise him up; and if he have committed sins, they shall be forgiven him.

James 5:14,15

Bless the Lord, O my soul, and forget not all his benefits: Who forgiveth all thine iniquities; who healeth all thy diseases.

Psalm 103:2,3

But Jesus turned him about, and when he saw her, he said, Daughter, be of good comfort; thy faith hath made thee whole. And the woman was made whole from that hour.

Matthew 9:22

And when he had called unto him his twelve disciples, he gave them power against unclean spirits, to cast them out, and to heal all manner of sickness and all manner of disease.

Matthew 10:1

Heal the sick, cleanse the lepers, raise the dead, cast out devils: freely ye have received, freely give.

Matthew 10:8

And God hath set some in the church, first apostles, secondarily prophets, thirdly teachers, after that miracles, then gifts of healings, helps, governments, diversitites of tongues.

I Corinthians 12:28

And the whole multitude sought to touch him: for there went virtue out of him, and healed them all.

Luke 6:19

And Jesus went about all Galilee, teaching in their synagogues, and preaching the gospel of the kingdom, and healing all manner of sickness and all manner of disease among the people.

Matthew 4:23

Additional Scripture References

Ex. 23:25; Deut. 32:39; Matt. 8:16,17; 19:2; Mark 7:32-35; 16:17,18; Luke 5:17; 6:17; Acts 3:6; 5:14-16; 8:6,7; 19:11,12; 28:8; I Cor. 12:7-12

Heaven

But as it is written, Eye hath not seen, nor ear heard, neither have entered into the heart of man, the things which God hath prepared for them that love him.

I Corinthians 2:9

He that hath an ear, let him hear what the Spirit saith unto the churches; To him that overcometh will I give to eat of the tree of life, which is in the midst of the paradise of God.

Revelation 2:7

For our conversation is in heaven; from whence also we look for the Saviour, the Lord Jesus Christ.

Philippians 3:20

Then hear thou in heaven thy dwelling-place.

I Kings 8:39

Blessed be the God and Father of our Lord Jesus Christ, which according to his abundant mercy hath begotten us again unto a lively hope by the resurrection of Jesus Christ from the dead, To an inheritance incorruptible, and undefiled, and that fadeth not away, reserved in heaven for you.

I Peter 1:3,4

Lay not up for yourselves treasures upon earth, where moth and rust doth corrupt, and where thieves break through and steal: But lay up for yourselves treasures in heaven, where neither moth nor rust doth corrupt, and where thieves do not break through nor steal.

Matthew 6:19-21

Heaven is my throne, and earth is my footstool: what house will ye build me? saith the Lord: or what is the place of my rest?

Acts 7:49

For ye had compassion of me in my bonds, and took joyfully the spoiling of your goods, knowing in yourselves that ye have in heaven a better and an enduring substance.

Hebrews 10:34

For Christ is not entered into the holy places made with hands, which are the figures of the true; but into heaven itself, now to appear in the presence of God for us.

Hebrews 9:24

For there are three that bear record in heaven, the Father, the Word, and the Holy Ghost: and these three are one.

I John 5:7

Additional Scripture References

Ps. 11:4; 113:5,6; Ecc. 5:2; Matt. 5:12; 6:9,10; 16:19; 18:10; Luke 23:43; John 3:12; 14:2,3; II Cor. 5:1; 12:2-4; Eph. 1:19-21; Rev. 5:13

Hell

And whosoever was not found written in the book of life was cast into the lake of fire.
Revelation 20:15

The wicked shall be turned into hell, and all the nations that forget God.
Psalm 9:17

So shall it be at the end of the world: the angels shall come forth, and sever the wicked from among the just, And shall cast them into the furnace of fire: there shall be wailing and gnashing of teeth.
Matthew 13:49,50

Ye serpents, ye generation of vipers, how can ye escape the damnation of hell?
Matthew 23:33

The sinners in Zion are afraid; fearfulness hath surprised the hypocrites. Who among us shall dwell with the devouring fire? who among us shall dwell with everlasting burnings?
Isaiah 33:14

Enter ye in at the strait gate: for wide is the gate, and broad is the way, that leadeth to destruction, and many there be which go in thereat.
Matthew 7:13

And the beast was taken, and with him the false prophet that wrought miracles before him, with which he deceived them that had received the mark of the beast, and them that worshipped his image. These both were cast alive into a lake of fire burning with brimstone.

Revelation 19:20

But the fearful, and unbelieving, and the abominable, and murderers, and whore-mongers, and sorcerers, and idolaters, and all liars, shall have their part in the lake which burneth with fire and brimstone: which is the second death.

Revelation 21:8

Therefore hell hath enlarged herself, and opened her mouth without measure: and their glory, and their multitude, and their pomp, and he that rejoiceth, shall descend into it.

Isaiah 5:14

And fear not them which kill the body, but are not able to kill the soul: but rather fear him which is able to destroy both soul and body in hell.

Matthew 10:28

Additional Scripture References

Prov. 9:13-18; Matt. 3:11,12; 13:41,42; 25:31-46; Luke 16:20-31; Acts 1:23-25; II Thes. 1:7-9; II Pet. 2:4; Rev. 14:9-11

Holiness

And one cried unto another, and said, Holy, holy, holy, is the Lord of hosts: the whole earth is full of his glory.

Isaiah 6:3

For God is the King of all the earth: sing ye praises with understanding. God reigneth over the heathen: God sitteth upon the throne of his holiness.

Psalm 47:7,8

But as he which hath called you is holy, so be ye holy in all manner of conversation; Because it is written, Be ye holy; for I am holy.

I Peter 1:15,16

Know ye not that ye are the temple of God, and that the Spirit of God dwelleth in you? If any man defile the temple of God, him shall God destroy; for the temple of God is holy, which temple ye are.

I Corinthians 3:16,17

Let no man despise thy youth; but be thou an example of the believers, in word, in conversation, in charity, in spirit, in faith, in purity.

I Timothy 4:12

And you, that were sometime alienated and enemies in your mind by wicked works, yet now hath he reconciled In the body of his flesh through death, to present you holy and unblameable and unreproveable in his sight.

Colossians 1:21,22

Let no man say when he is tempted, I am tempted of God: for God cannot be tempted with evil, neither tempteth he any man.

James 1:13

Follow peace with all men, and holiness, without which no man shall see the Lord.

Hebrews 12:14

That he might present it to himself a glorious church, not having spot, or wrinkle, or any such thing; but that it should be holy and without blemish.

Ephesians 5:27

Having therefore these promises, dearly beloved, let us cleanse ourselves from all filthiness of the flesh and spirit, perfecting holiness in the fear of God.

II Corinthians 7:1

Additional Scripture References

Ex. 3:1-6; Lev. 11:44; 19:1,2; 20:26; Ps. 22:3; 30:4; 111:9; 145:17; Matt. 5:48; Rom. 6:1-23; Eph. 1:4; I Thes. 4:7; I Tim. 6:11; II Tim. 2:19-22; II Pet. 1:5-11; I Jn. 2:5,6; Rev. 4:8; 20:6

Honoring the Poor

Blessed is he that considereth the poor: the Lord will deliver him in time of trouble. The Lord will preserve him, and keep him alive; and he shall be blessed upon the earth: and thou wilt not deliver him unto the will of his enemies. The Lord will strengthen him upon the bed of languishing: thou wilt make all his bed in his sickness.

Psalm 41:1-3

He that hath pity upon the poor lendeth unto the Lord; and that which he hath given will he pay him again.

Proverbs 19:17

He that oppresseth the poor reproacheth his Maker: but he that honoureth him hath mercy on the poor.

Proverbs 14:31

For the poor shall never cease out of the land: therefore I command thee, saying, Thou shalt open thine hand wide unto thy brother, to thy poor, and to thy needy, in thy land.

Deuteronomy 15:11

But whoso hath this world's good, and seeth his brother have need, and shutteth up his bowels of compassion from him, how dwelleth the love of God in him?

I John 3:17

And the King shall answer and say unto them, Verily I say unto you, Inasmuch as ye have done it unto one of the least of these my brethren, ye have done it unto me.

Matthew 25:40

Whoso stoppeth his ears at the cry of the poor, he also shall cry himself, but shall not be heard.

Proverbs 21:13

He that giveth unto the poor shall not lack: but he that hideth his eyes shall have many a curse.

Proverbs 28:27

He answereth and saith unto them, He that hath two coats, let him impart to him that hath none; and he that hath meat, let him do likewise.

Luke 3:11

Additional Scripture References

Lev. 25:35; Deut. 15:7,8; I Sam. 2:7,8; Ps. 12:5; 72:12-14; 109:31; Prov. 14:21; 29:7; Matt. 5:42; 25:34-36; Luke 14:12-14; 18:22; Acts 20:35; II Cor. 9:6; Gal. 6:9,10; James 2:1-9; 2:14-16

Hope

Behold, the eye of the Lord is upon them that fear him, upon them that hope in his mercy.

Psalm 33:18

To whom God would make known what is the riches of the glory of this mystery among the Gentiles; which is Christ in you, the hope of glory.

Colossians 1:27

Blessed be the God and Father of our Lord Jesus Christ, which according to his abundant mercy hath begotten us again unto a lively hope by the resurrection of Jesus Christ from the dead.

I Peter 1:3

And every man that hath this hope in him purifieth himself, even as he is pure.

I John 3:3

Or saith he it altogether for our sakes? For our sakes, no doubt, this is written: that he that ploweth should plow in hope; and that he that thresheth in hope should be partaker of his hope.

I Corinthians 9:10

It is good that a man should both hope and quietly wait for the salvation of the Lord.

Lamentations 3:26

Happy is he that hath the God of Jacob for his help, whose hope is in the Lord his God.

Psalm 146:5

By whom also we have access by faith into this grace wherein we stand, and rejoice in hope of the glory of God.

Romans 5:2

Paul, an apostle of Jesus Christ by the commandment of God our Saviour, and Lord Jesus Christ, which is our hope.

I Timothy 1:1

Additional Scripture References

Job 11:18; 11:20; 14:7; 27:8-10; Ps. 147:11; Prov. 11:7; 13:12; Jer. 17:7,8; Acts 26:6; Rom. 5:5; 15:4; 15:13; I Cor. 13:13; Gal. 5:5; Eph. 2:12; Col. 1:5; I Thes. 4:13; Titus 2:13; Heb. 6:18,19; I Pet. 3:15

Humility

For thus saith the high and lofty One that inhabiteth eternity, whose name is Holy; I dwell in the high and holy place, with him also that is of a contrite and humble spirit, to revive the spirit of the humble, and to revive the heart of the contrite ones.

Isaiah 57:15

For whosoever exalteth himself shall be abased; and he that humbleth himself shall be exalted.

Luke 14:11

He hath shewed thee, O man, what is good; and what doth the Lord require of thee, but to do justly, and to love mercy, and to walk humbly with thy God?

Micah 6:8

And thou shalt remember that thou wast a bondman in the land of Egypt, and the Lord thy God redeemed thee: therefore I command thee this thing to day.

Deuteronomy 15:15

Let another man praise thee, and not thine own mouth; a stranger, and not thine own lips.

Proverbs 27:2

By humility and the fear of the Lord are riches, and honour, and life.

Proverbs 22:4

The sacrifices of God are a broken spirit: a broken and a contrite heart, O God, thou wilt not despise.

Psalm 51:17

But God forbid that I should glory, save in the cross of our Lord Jesus Christ, by whom the world is crucified unto me, and I unto the world.

Galatians 6:14

. . . Wherefore he saith, God resisteth the proud, but giveth grace unto the humble.

James 4:6

For I say, through the grace given unto me, to every man that is among you, not to think of himself more highly than he ought to think; but to think soberly, according as God hath dealt to every man the measure of faith.

Romans 12:3

Additional Scripture References

Ps. 138:6; Prov. 3:34; 11:2; 15:33; 16:19; 25:6,7; 29:23; Matt. 5:3; 18:2-4; Luke 10:21; John 3:30; I Cor. 10:12; Phil. 2:3-11; Col. 3:12-14; James 4:10; I Pet. 5:5,6

Idolatry

I am the Lord thy God, which brought thee out of the land of Egypt, from the house of bondage. Thou shalt have none other gods before me.

Deuteronomy 5:6,7

Mortify therefore your members which are upon the earth; fornication, uncleanness, inordinate affection, evil concupiscence, and covetousness, which is idolatry: For which things' sake the wrath of God cometh on the children of disobedience.

Colossians 3:5,6

For the Lord is great, and greatly to be praised: he is to be feared above all gods. For all the gods of the nations are idols: but the Lord made the heavens. Honour and majesty are before him: strength and beauty are in his sanctuary.

Psalm 96:4-6

Then saith Jesus unto him, Get thee hence, Satan: for it is written, Thou shalt worship the Lord thy God, and him only shalt thou serve.

Matthew 4:10

They made a calf in Horeb, and worshipped the molten image. Thus they changed their glory into the similitude of an ox that eateth grass.

Psalm 106:19,20

And the loftiness of man shall be bowed down, and the haughtiness of men shall be made low: and the Lord alone shall be exalted in that day. And the idols he shall utterly abolish.

Isaiah 2:17,18

But the fearful, and unbelieving, and the abominable, and murderers, and whoremongers, and sorcerers, and idolaters, and all liars, shall have their part in the lake which burneth with fire and brimstone: which is the second death.

Revelation 21:8

Blessed are they that do his commandments, that they may have right to the tree of life, and may enter in through the gates into the city. For without are dogs, and sorcerers, and whoremongers, and murderers, and idolaters, and whosoever loveth and maketh a lie.

Revelation 22:14,15

Additional Scripture References

Ex. 23:13; 34:14; Lev. 19:4; Deut. 4:15-24; Josh. 24:14-25; II Chr. 28:22,23; Is. 37:18,19; 40:12-26; 44:6-20; Jer. 2:26-28; Ezek. 8:8-18; 14:2-8; Acts 17:22-31; Rom. 1:16-32; I Cor. 5:9-13; 6:9,10; 8:1-6; Gal. 4:8,9; I Jn. 5:21

Joy of the Lord

Thou wilt shew me the path of life: in thy presence is fulness of joy; at thy right hand there are pleasures for evermore.

Psalm 16:11

Be glad in the Lord, and rejoice, ye righteous: and shout for joy, all ye that are upright in heart.

Psalm 32:11

Therefore with joy shall ye draw water out of the wells of salvation.

Isaiah 12:3

Restore unto me the joy of thy salvation; and uphold me with thy free spirit.

Psalm 51:12

Therefore the redeemed of the Lord shall return, and come with singing unto Zion; and everlasting joy shall be upon their head: they shall obtain gladness and joy; and sorrow and mourning shall flee away.

Isaiah 51:11

His lord said unto him, Well done, thou good and faithful servant: thou hast been faithful over a few things, I will make thee ruler over many things: enter thou into the joy of thy lord.

Matthew 25:21

For God giveth to a man that is good in his sight wisdom, and knowledge, and joy.

Ecclesiastes 2:26

These things have I spoken unto you, that my joy might remain in you, and that your joy might be full.

John 15:11

Hitherto have ye asked nothing in my name: ask, and ye shall receive, that your joy may be full.

John 16:24

But the fruit of the Spirit is love, joy, peace, longsuffering, gentleness, goodness, faith.

Galatians 5:22

Additional Scripture References

Ps. 21:1; 43:4; Ecc. 5:19,20; Is. 29:19; 61:3; 61:7; Hab. 3:18; Zeph. 3:17; Luke 1:14; 15:10; John 16:20-22; Acts 13:52; 15:3; 20:24; Rom. 5:11; 14:17; II Cor. 1:24; I Thes. 1:6; I Pet. 1:8

Judgment

For we must all appear before the judgment seat of Christ; that every one may receive the things done in his body, according to that he hath done, whether it be good or bad.

II Corinthians 5:10

Be not deceived; God is not mocked: for whatsoever a man soweth, that shall he also reap. For he that soweth to his flesh shall of the flesh reap corruption; but he that soweth to the Spirit shall of the Spirit reap life everlasting.

Galatians 6:7,8

For God shall bring every work into judgment, with every secret thing, whether it be good, or whether it be evil.

Ecclesiastes 12:14

And I saw the dead, small and great, stand before God; and the books were opened: and another book was opened, which is the book of life: and the dead were judged out of those things which were written in the books, according to their works.

Revelation 20:12

But I say unto you, That every idle word that men shall speak, they shall give account thereof in the day of judgment. For by thy words thou shalt be justified, and by thy words thou shalt be condemned.

Matthew 12:36,37

For the Son of man shall come in the glory of his Father with his angels; and then he shall reward every man according to his works.

Matthew 16:27

I the Lord search the heart, I try the reins, even to give every man according to his ways, and according to the fruit of his doings.

Jeremiah 17:10

So speak ye, and so do, as they that shall be judged by the law of liberty. For he shall have judgment without mercy, that hath shewed no mercy; and mercy rejoiceth against judgment.

James 2:12,13

For there is nothing covered, that shall not be revealed; neither hid, that shall not be known.

Luke 12:2

Additional Scripture References

Ps. 9:7,8; 62:12; 128:1,2; Ecc. 11:9; Is. 3:10,11; Jer. 32:17-19; Ezek. 7:1-4; Matt. 13:24-30, 13:37-43; 25:31-46; Mark 8:38; Luke 13:24-29; 19:12-27; Rom. 2:1-12; 14:10; I Cor. 3:8; 3:13-15; Col. 3:23-25; II Thes. 1:3-10; II Tim. 4:7,8; Heb. 10:26-31; Rev. 22:12

Justification

But God commendeth his love toward us, in that, while we were yet sinners, Christ died for us. Much more then, being now justified by his blood, we shall be saved from wrath through him.

Romans 5:8,9

Therefore as by the offence of one judgment came upon all men to condemnation; even so by the rightousness of one the free gift came upon all men unto justification of life.

Romans 5:18

And such were some of you: but ye are washed, but ye are sanctified, but ye are justified in the name of the Lord Jesus, and by the Spirit of our God.

I Corinthians 6:11

Knowing that a man is not justified by the works of the law, but by the faith of Jesus Christ, even we have believed in Jesus Christ, that we might be justified by the faith of Christ, and not by the works of the law: for by the works of the law shall no flesh be justified.

Galatians 2:16

Moreover whom he did predestinate, them he also called: and whom he called, them he also justified: and whom he justified, them he also glorified.

Romans 8:30

Verily, verily, I say unto you, He that heareth my word, and believeth on him that sent me, hath everlasting life, and shall not come into condemnation; but is passed from death unto life.

John 5:24

Be it known unto you therefore, men and brethren, that through this man is preached unto you the forgiveness of sins: And by him all that believe are justified from all things, from which ye could not be justified by the law of Moses.

Acts 13:38,39

Therefore we conclude that a man is justified by faith without the deeds of the law.

Romans 3:28

Therefore being justified by faith, we have peace with God through our Lord Jesus Christ: By whom also we have access by faith into this grace wherein we stand, and rejoice in hope of the glory of God.

Romans 5:1,2

Additional Scripture References

Ps. 32:1,2; Is. 53:1-12; Rom. 3:19-26; 4:1-25; Gal. 3:24; Phil. 3:7-10; Titus 3:4-7

Kingdom of God

Thine, O Lord, is the greatness, and the power, and the glory, and the victory, and the majesty: for all that is in the heaven and in the earth is thine; thine is the kingdom, O Lord, and thou art exalted as head above all.

I Chronicles 29:11

All thy works shall praise thee, O Lord; and thy saints shall bless thee. They shall speak of the glory of thy kingdom, and talk of thy power; To make known to the sons of men his mighty acts, and the glorious majesty of his kingdom. Thy kingdom is an everlasting kingdom, and thy dominion endureth throughout all generations.

Psalm 145:10-13

The Lord hath prepared his throne in the heavens; and his kingdom ruleth over all.

Psalm 103:19

The Lord is King for ever and ever: the heathen are perished out of his land.

Psalm 10:16

And in the days of these kings shall the God of heaven set up a kingdom, which shall never be destroyed: and the kingdom shall not be left to other people, but it shall break in pieces and consume all these kingdoms, and it shall stand for ever.

Daniel 2:44

And there was given him dominion, and glory, and a kingdom, that all people, nations, and languages, should serve him: his dominion is an everlasting dominion, which shall not pass away, and his kingdom that which shall not be destroyed.

Daniel 7:14

All the ends of the world shall remember and turn unto the Lord: and all the kindreds of the nations shall worship before thee. For the kingdom is the Lord's: and he is the governor among the nations.

Psalm 22:27,28

And the kingdom and dominion, and the greatness of the kingdom under the whole heaven, shall be given to the people of the saints of the most High, whose kingdom is an everlasting kingdom, and all dominions shall serve and obey him.

Daniel 7:27

And at the end of the days I Nebuchadnezzar lifted up mine eyes unto heaven, and mine understanding returned unto me, and I blessed the most High, and I praised and honoured him that liveth for ever, whose dominion is an everlasting dominion, and his kingdom is from generation to generation.

Daniel 4:34

Kingdom of Heaven

From that time Jesus began to preach, and to say, Repent: for the kingdom of heaven is at hand.

Matthew 4:17

Again, the kingdom of heaven is like unto treasure hid in a field; the which when a man hath found, he hideth, and for joy thereof goeth and selleth all that he hath, and buyeth that field.

Matthew 13:44

Fear not, little flock; for it is your Father's good pleasure to give you the kingdom.

Luke 12:32

Jesus answered and said unto him, Verily, verily, I say unto thee, Except a man be born again, he cannot see the kingdom of God . . . Jesus answered, Verily, verily, I say unto thee, Except a man be born of water and of the Spirit, he cannot enter into the kingdom of God.

John 3:3,5

For this ye know, that no whoremonger, nor unclean person, nor covetous man, who is an idolater, hath any inheritance in the kingdom of Christ and of God.

Ephesians 5:5

Now this I say, brethren, that flesh and blood cannot inherit the kingdom of God; neither doth corruption inherit incorruption.

I Corinthians 15:50

And Jesus said unto him, No man, having put his hand to the plough, and looking back, is fit for the kingdom of God.

Luke 9:62

Verily I say unto you, Whosoever shall not receive the kingdom of God as a little child, he shall not enter therein.

Mark 10:15

And it came to pass afterward, that he went throughout every city and village, preaching and shewing the glad tidings of the kingdom of God: and the twelve were with him.

Luke 8:1

But seek ye first the kingdom of God, and his righteousness; and all these things shall be added unto you.

Matthew 6:33

For the kingdom of God is not meat and drink; but righteousness, and peace, and joy in the Holy Ghost.

Romans 14:17

Additional Scripture References

Matt. 3:1,2; 12:28; 13:13-33; 13:45-48; 25:1-13; 25:14-46; Mark 4:11; 4:30-32; 10:23-25; Luke 1:33; 9:60; 10:9; 17:20,21; John 18:36; Acts 14:22; I Cor. 4:20; 6:9-11

Knowledge

O the depth of the riches both of the wisdom and knowledge of God! how unsearchable are his judgments, and his ways past finding out!

Romans 11:33

There is gold, and a multitude of rubies: but the lips of knowledge are a precious jewel.

Proverbs 20:15

The heavens declare the glory of God; and the firmament sheweth his handiwork. Day unto day uttereth speech, and night unto night sheweth knowledge. There is no speech nor language, where their voice is not heard.

Psalm 19:1-3

Receive my instruction, and not silver; and knowledge rather than choice gold.

Proverbs 8:10

For God, who commanded the light to shine out of darkness, hath shined in our hearts, to give the light of the knowledge of the glory of God in the face of Jesus Christ.

II Corinthians 4:6

But what things were gain to me, those I counted loss for Christ. Yea doubtless, and I count all things but loss for the excellency of the knowledge of Christ Jesus my Lord: for whom I have suffered the loss of all things, and do count them but dung, that I may win Christ.

Philippians 3:7,8

The fear of the Lord is the beginning of knowledge: but fools despise wisdom and instruction.

Proverbs 1:7

Through wisdom is an house builded; and by understanding it is established: And by knowledge shall the chambers be filled with all precious and pleasant riches.

Proverbs 24:3,4

And I will give you pastors according to mine heart, which shall feed you with knowledge and understanding.

Jeremiah 3:15

And wisdom and knowledge shall be the stability of thy times, and strength of salvation: the fear of the Lord is his treasure.

Isaiah 33:6

Additional Scripture References

II Chr. 1:11,12; Prov. 2:6; 9:10; 10:14; 11:9; 14:18; 15:14; 18:15; 22:17; Dan. 2:20-23; Hos. 6:6; I Cor. 1:3-8; II Cor. 6:1-10; Eph. 1:15-23

Knowledge (Lack Of)

My people are destroyed for lack of knowledge: because thou hast rejected knowledge, I will also reject thee, that thou shalt be no priest to me: seeing thou hast forgotten the law of thy God, I will also forget thy children.

Hosea 4:6

Awake to righteousness, and sin not; for some have not the knowledge of God: I speak this to your shame.

I Corinthians 15:34

Ever learning, and never able to come to the knowledge of the truth.

II Timothy 3:7

Go from the presence of a foolish man, when thou perceivest not in him the lips of knowledge.

Proverbs 14:7

Assemble yourselves and come; draw near together, ye that are escaped of the nations: they have no knowledge that set up the wood of their graven image, and pray unto a god that cannot save.

Isaiah 45:20

For my people is foolish, they have not known me; they are sottish children, and they have none understanding: they are wise to do evil, but to do good they have no knowledge.

Jeremiah 4:22

Therefore my people are gone into captivity, because they have no knowledge: and their honourable men are famished, and their multitude dried up with thirst.

Isaiah 5:13

Then shall they call upon me, but I will not answer; they shall seek me early, but they shall not find me: For that they hated knowledge, and did not choose the fear of the Lord.

Proverbs 1:28,29

How long, ye simple ones, will ye love simplicity? and the scorners delight in their scorning, and fools hate knowledge?

Proverbs 1:22

Who is this that darkeneth counsel by words without knowledge?

Job 38:2

Have all the workers of iniquity no knowledge? who eat up my people as they eat bread, and call not upon the Lord.

Psalm 14:4

Therefore they say unto God, Depart from us; for we desire not the knowledge of thy ways.

Job 21:14

Love

And now abideth faith, hope, charity, these three; but the greatest of these is charity.
I Corinthians 13:13

Thou shalt not avenge, nor bear any grudge against the children of thy people, but thou shalt love thy neighbour as thyself: I am the Lord.
Leviticus 19:18

Though I speak with the tongues of men and of angels, and have not charity, I am become as sounding brass, or a tinkling cymbal.
I Corinthians 13:1

For all the law is fulfilled in one word, even in this; Thou shalt love thy neighbour as thyself.
Galatians 5:14

But thou, O man of God, flee these things; and follow after righteousness, godliness, faith, love, patience, meekness.
I Timothy 6:11

And above all things have fervent charity among yourselves: for charity shall cover the multitude of sins.
I Peter 4:8

But the fruit of the Spirit is love, joy, peace, longsuffering, gentleness, goodness, faith, Meekness, temperance: against such there is no law.
Galatians 5:22,23

By this shall all men know that ye are my disciples, if ye have love one to another.

John 13:35

Beloved, let us love one another: for love is of God; and every one that loveth is born of God, and knoweth God. He that loveth not knoweth not God; for God is love.

I John 4:7,8

And above all these things put on charity, which is the bond of perfectness.

Colossians 3:14

Additional Scripture References

Prov. 10:12; Matt. 5:43-47; 22:37-40;
John 15:12,13; Rom. 13:10; I Cor. 13:1-13;
16:14; Gal. 5:13; Eph. 3:14-19; 4:1-32; 5:1,2;
Phil. 2:2; I Tim. 1:5; 4:12; Titus 2:1,2;
Heb. 10:24; II Pet. 1:2-11; I Jn. 2:5; 4:7-21

Loving God

And thou shalt love the Lord thy God with all thine heart, and with all thy soul, and with all thy might.

Deuteronomy 6:5

Because he hath set his love upon me, therefore will I deliver him: I will set him on high, because he hath known my name.

Psalm 91:14

But as it is written, Eye hath not seen, nor ear heard, neither have entered into the heart of man, the things which God hath prepared for them that love him.

I Corinthians 2:9

We love him, because he first loved us.

I John 4:19

I love the Lord, because he hath heard my voice and my supplications.

Psalm 116:1

He that hath my commandments, and keepeth them, he it is that loveth me: and he that loveth me shall be loved of my Father, and I will love him, and will manifest myself to him.

John 14:21

And we know that all things work together for good to them that love God, to them who are the called according to his purpose.

Romans 8:28

But if any man love God, the same is known of him.

I Corinthians 8:3

He that loveth father or mother more than me is not worthy of me: and he that loveth son or daughter more than me is not worthy of me.

Matthew 10:37

For God will save Zion, and will build the cities of Judah: that they may dwell there, and have it in possession. The seed also of his servants shall inherit it: and they that love his name shall dwell therein.

Psalm 69:35,36

Additional Scripture References

Neh. 1:4,5; Ps. 31:23; 145:20;
Matt. 22:37-40; John 6:28,29; 14:23,24;
James 1:12; I Jn. 5:1-3

Lust

For all that is in the world, the lust of the flesh, and the lust of the eyes, and the pride of life, is not of the Father, but is of the world. And the world passeth away, and the lust thereof: but he that doeth the will of God abideth for ever.

I John 2:16,17

And the cares of this world, and the deceitfulness of riches, and the lusts of other things entering in, choke the word, and it becometh unfruitful.

Mark 4:19

But every man is tempted, when he is drawn away of his own lust, and enticed. Then when lust hath conceived, it bringeth forth sin: and sin, when it is finished, bringeth forth death.

James 1:14,15

But put ye on the Lord Jesus Christ, and make not provision for the flesh, to fulfil the lusts thereof.

Romans 13:14

For the grace of God that bringeth salvation hath appeared to all men, Teaching us that, denying ungodliness and worldly lusts, we should live soberly, righteously, and godly, in this present world.

Titus 2:11,12

Whereby are given unto us exceeding great and precious promises: that by these ye might be partakers of the divine nature, having escaped the corruption that is in the world through lust.

II Peter 1:4

And God saw that the wickedness of man was great in the earth, and that every imagination of the thoughts of his heart was only evil continually. And it repented the Lord that he had made man on the earth, and it grieved him at his heart.

Genesis 6:5,6

Let not sin therefore reign in your mortal body, that ye should obey it in the lusts thereof.

Romans 6:12

Dearly beloved, I beseech you as strangers and pilgrims, abstain from fleshly lusts, which war against the soul.

I Peter 2:11

Additional Scripture References

Gen. 3:6; Ex. 20:17; Ps. 78:9-19; 81:10-16; Prov. 6:20-29; Matt. 5:27,28; Rom. 7:23; I Cor. 10:1-6; Gal. 5:16-17; Eph. 2:1-7; 4:17-32; Col. 3:5; I Thes. 4:3-7; I Tim. 6:9; II Tim. 2:22; 4:1-4; Titus 3:3-7

Lying - Deceitfulness

These six things doth the Lord hate: yea, seven are an abomination unto him: A proud look, a lying tongue, and hands that shed innocent blood, An heart that deviseth wicked imaginations, feet that be swift in running to mischief, A false witness that speaketh lies, and he that soweth discord among brethren.

Proverbs 6:16-19

Let not mercy and truth forsake thee: bind them about thy neck; write them upon the table of thine heart: So shalt thou find favour and good understanding in the sight of God and man.

Proverbs 3:3,4

Ye are of your father the devil, and the lusts of your father ye will do. He was a murderer from the beginning, and abode not in the truth, because there is no truth in him. When he speaketh a lie, he speaketh of his own: for he is a liar, and the father of it.

John 8:44

He that worketh deceit shall not dwell within my house: he that telleth lies shall not tarry in my sight.

Psalm 101:7

But the fearful, and unbelieving, and the abominable, and murderers, and whoremongers, and sorcerers, and idolaters, and all liars, shall have their part in the lake which burneth with fire and brimstone: which is the second death.

Revelation 21:8

Lie not one to another, seeing that ye have put off the old man with his deeds; And have put on the new man, which is renewed in knowledge after the image of him that created him.

Colossians 3:9,10

Wherefore putting away lying, speak every man truth with his neighbour: for we are members one of another.

Ephesians 4:25

Blessed is that man that maketh the Lord his trust, and respecteth not the proud, nor such as turn aside to lies.

Psalm 40:4

A false witness shall not be unpunished, and he that speaketh lies shall perish.

Proverbs 19:9

Additional Scripture References

Lev. 19:11; Ps. 31:6; 119:29,30; 119:161-168; 120:2; Prov. 12:17-19; 13:5; 17:4; 20:17; 21:6; Jer. 9:1-9; 23:14-32; Ezek. 13:1-16; Hos. 4:1-5; II Cor. 4:1,2; Eph. 4:29; I Jn. 2:3,4; 2:22; 4:20

Man's Carnal Nature

The heart is deceitful above all things, and desperately wicked: who can know it?

Jeremiah 17:9

Because the carnal mind is enmity against God: for it is not subject to the law of God, neither indeed can be. So then they that are in the flesh cannot please God. But ye are not in the flesh, but in the Spirit, if so be that the Spirit of God dwell in you. Now if any man have not the Spirit of Christ, he is none of his.

Romans 8:7-9

But the natural man receiveth not the things of the Spirit of God: for they are foolishness unto him: neither can he know them, because they are spiritually discerned.

I Corinthians 2:14

That which is born of the flesh is flesh; and that which is born of the Spirit is spirit.

John 3:6

And they that are Christ's have crucified the flesh with the affections and lusts.

Galatians 5:24

And the Lord smelled a sweet savour; and the Lord said in his heart, I will not again curse the ground any more for man's sake; for the imagination of man's heart is evil from his youth; neither will I again smite any more every thing living, as I have done.

Genesis 8:21

Behold, I was shapen in iniquity; and in sin did my mother conceive me.

Psalm 51:5

Among whom also we all had our conversation in times past in the lusts of our flesh, fulfilling the desires of the flesh and of the mind; and were by nature the children of wrath, even as others.

Ephesians 2:3

But he turned, and said unto Peter, Get thee behind me, Satan: thou art an offence unto me: for thou savourest not the things that be of God, but those that be of men.

Matthew 16:23

And that ye put on the new man, which after God is created in righteousness and true holiness.

Ephesians 4:24

Additional Scripture References

Gen. 6:5; Ps. 14:1-3; Matt. 26:41; Rom. 3:10; 8:5; 8:13; I Cor. 15:39; II Cor. 7:1; Gal. 5:17; 19-23; I Pet. 1:24; I Jn. 2:15,16

Marriage

And the Lord God said, It is not good that the man should be alone; I will make him an help meet for him.

Genesis 2:18

Therefore shall a man leave his father and his mother, and shall cleave unto his wife: and they shall be one flesh.

Genesis 2:24

And he answered and said unto them, Have ye not read, that he which made them at the beginning made them male and female, And said, For this cause shall a man leave father and mother, and shall cleave to his wife: and they twain shall be one flesh? Wherefore they are no more twain, but one flesh. What therefore God hath joined together, let not man put asunder.

Matthew 19:4-6

Let thy fountain be blessed: and rejoice with the wife of thy youth. Let her be as the loving hind and pleasant roe; let her breasts satisfy thee at all times; and be thou ravished always with her love.

Proverbs 5:18,19

Wives, submit yourselves unto your own husbands, as it is fit in the Lord. Husbands, love your wives, and be not bitter against them.

Colossians 3:18,19

Likewise, ye husbands, dwell with them according to knowledge, giving honour unto the wife, as unto the weaker vessel, and as being heirs together of the grace of life; that your prayers be not hindered.

I Peter 3:7

For the husband is the head of the wife, even as Christ is the head of the church: and he is the saviour of the body.

Ephesians 5:23

Likewise, ye wives, be in subjection to your own husbands; that, if any obey not the word, they also may without the word be won by the conversation of the wives; While they behold your chaste conversation coupled with fear.

I Peter 3:1,2

Whoso findeth a wife findeth a good thing, and obtaineth favour of the Lord.

Proverbs 18:22

Additional Scripture References

Matt. 5:31,32; Rom. 7:1-3; I Cor. 7:1-17; 7:25-40; 11:3; Eph. 5:22-33; Heb. 13:4

Missions

Go ye therefore, and teach all nations, baptizing them in the name of the Father, and of the Son, and of the Holy Ghost: Teaching them to observe all things whatsoever I have commanded you: and, lo, I am with you alway, even unto the end of the world. Amen.

Matthew 28:19,20

. . . and ye shall be witnesses unto me both in Jerusalem, and in all Judaea, and in Samaria, and unto the uttermost part of the earth.

Acts 1:8

And that repentance and remission of sins should be preached in his name among all nations, beginning at Jerusalem.

Luke 24:47

And they that be wise shall shine as the brightness of the firmament; and they that turn many to righteousness as the stars for ever and ever.

Daniel 12:3

Sing unto the Lord, all the earth; shew forth from day to day his salvation. Declare his glory among the heathen; his marvellous works among all nations.

I Chronicles 16:23,24

As every man hath received the gift, even so minister the same one to another, as good stewards of the manifold grace of God.

I Peter 4:10

And Jesus said unto them, Come ye after me, and I will make you to become fishers of men.

Mark 1:17

But if our gospel be hid, it is hid to them that are lost.

II Corinthians 4:3

Let your light so shine before men, that they may see your good works, and glorify your Father which is in heaven.

Matthew 5:16

Whosoever therefore shall confess me before men, him will I confess also before my Father which is in heaven.

Matthew 10:32

Additional Scripture References

Deut. 6:6-9; Ps. 18:49; 51:12,13; 71:17,18; 77:12; 78:5-8; 96:1-13; 119:10-12; 119:46; Luke 19:37-40; Eph. 4:29; Phil. 2:14,15; Col. 4:6; I Thes. 5:14; I Pet. 2:11-15

Murmuring

Do all things without murmurings and disputings.

Philippians 2:14

Curse not the king, no not in thy thought; and curse not the rich in thy bedchamber: for a bird of the air shall carry the voice, and that which hath wings shall tell the matter.

Ecclesiastes 10:20

Therefore hath he mercy on whom he will have mercy, and whom he will he hardeneth. Thou wilt say then unto me, Why doth he yet find fault? For who hath resisted his will? Nay but, O man, who art thou that repliest against God? Shall the thing formed say to him that formed it, Why hast thou made me thus?

Romans 9:18-20

And the people spake against God, and against Moses, Wherefore have ye brought us up out of Egypt to die in the wilderness? for there is no bread, neither is there any water; and our soul loatheth this light bread. And the Lord sent fiery serpents among the people, and they bit the people; and much people of Israel died.

Numbers 21:5,6

And there was much murmuring among the people concerning him: for some said, He is a good man: others said, Nay; but he deceiveth the people.

John 7:12

Neither murmur ye, as some of them also murmured, and were destroyed of the destroyer.

I Corinthians 10:10

The foolishness of man perverteth his way: and his heart fretteth against the Lord.

Proverbs 19:3

Say not thou, What is the cause that the former days were better than these? for thou dost not enquire wisely concerning this.

Ecclesiastes 7:10

But on the morrow all the congregation of the children of Israel murmured against Moses and against Aaron, saying, Ye have killed the people of the Lord.

Numbers 16:41

The Jews then murmured at him, because he said, I am the bread which came down from heaven.

John 6:41

Additional Scripture References

Ex. 16:1-18; Num. 11:1-35; 14:26-37; 17:1-10; 20:1-12; Deut. 1:27; Ps. 106:4-48; Is. 29:23,24

The New Man

Therefore if any man be in Christ, he is a new creature: old things are passed away; behold, all things are become new.

II Corinthians 5:17

Lie not one to another, seeing that ye have put off the old man with his deeds; And have put on the new man, which is renewed in knowledge after the image of him that created him.

Colossians 3:9,10

And such were some of you: but ye are washed, but ye are sanctified, but ye are justified in the name of the Lord Jesus, and by the Spirit of our God.

I Corinthians 6:11

But ye are not in the flesh, but in the Spirit, if so be that the Spirit of God dwell in you. Now if any man have not the Spirit of Christ, he is none of his. And if Christ be in you, the body is dead because of sin; but the Spirit is life because of righteousness.

Romans 8:9,10

But we all, with open face beholding as in a glass the glory of the Lord, are changed into the same image from glory to glory, even as by the Spirit of the Lord.

II Corinthians 3:18

Whereby are given unto us exceeding

great and precious promises: that by these ye might be partakers of the divine nature, having escaped the corruption that is in the world through lust.

II Peter 1:4

A new heart also will I give you, and a new spirit will I put within you: and I will take away the stony heart out of your flesh, and I will give you an heart of flesh.

Ezekiel 36:26

I am crucified with Christ: nevertheless I live; yet not I, but Christ liveth in me: and the life which I now live in the flesh I live by the faith of the Son of God, who loved me, and gave himself for me.

Galatians 2:20

Being confident of this very thing, that he which hath begun a good work in you will perform it until the day of Jesus Christ.

Philippians 1:6

Additional Scripture References

I Kin. 8:57,58; Ps. 51:10; John 6:56,57; 8:12; 14:23; 15:3; Rom. 6:6; 7:5,6; 8:1-13; 8:29; 12:2; I Cor. 2:1-16; 4:6,7; Gal. 5:24-26; Eph. 2:1-13; 4:17-24; Col. 3:1-10; I Pet. 2:9

Obedience to God

He that hath my commandments, and keepeth them, he it is that loveth me: and he that loveth me shall be loved of my Father, and I will love him, and will manifest myself to him.

John 14:21

For whosoever shall do the will of my Father which is in heaven, the same is my brother, and sister, and mother.

Matthew 12:50

Know ye not, that to whom ye yield yourselves servants to obey, his servants ye are to whom ye obey; whether of sin unto death, or of obedience unto righteousness?

Romans 6:16

Let us hear the conclusion of the whole matter: Fear God, and keep his commandments: for this is the whole duty of man.

Ecclesiastes 12:13

But the mercy of the Lord is from everlasting to everlasting upon them that fear him, and his righteousness unto children's children.

Psalm 103:17

And the world passeth away, and the lust thereof: but he that doeth the will of God abideth for ever.

I John 2:17

And hereby we do know that we know

him, if we keep his commandments. He that saith, I know him, and keepeth not his commandments, is a liar, and the truth is not in him. But whoso keepeth his word, in him verily is the love of God perfected: hereby know we that we are in him. He that saith he abideth in him ought himself also so to walk, even as he walked.

I John 2:3-6

And Samuel said, Hath the Lord as great delight in burnt offerings and sacrifices, as in obeying the voice of the Lord? Behold, to obey is better than sacrifice, and to hearken than the fat of rams.

I Samuel 15:22

My son, forget not my law; but let thine heart keep my commandments: For length of days, and long life, and peace, shall they add to thee.

Proverbs 3:1,2

Additional Scripture References

Gen. 17:9; Lev. 19:37; Deut. 7:9; 10:12; Josh. 1:8; Ps. 119:2; Prov. 16:7; Jer. 7:23; 26:13; Matt. 3:15; 7:24-27; John 8:51;14:15; 15:10; Acts 24:16; Rom. 13:1,2; Heb. 5:8,9; James 1:22-25; I Pet. 1:13-16; 4:16,17; II Jn. 9

Our Needs Provided

But my God shall supply all your need according to his riches in glory by Christ Jesus.

Philippians 4:19

The Lord is my shepherd; I shall not want.

Psalm 23:1

Be careful for nothing; but in every thing by prayer and supplication with thanksgiving let your requests be made known unto God. And the peace of God, which passeth all understanding, shall keep your hearts and minds through Christ Jesus.

Philippians 4:6,7

Therefore I say unto you, Take no thought for your life, what ye shall eat, or what ye shall drink; nor yet for your body, what ye shall put on. Is not the life more than meat, and the body than raiment? Behold the fowls of the air: for they sow not, neither do they reap, nor gather into barns; yet your heavenly Father feedeth them. Are ye not much better than they?

Matthew 6:25,26

Every moving thing that liveth shall be meat for you; even as the green herb have I given you all things.

Genesis 9:3

He causeth the grass to grow for the cattle, and herb for the service of man: that he may bring forth food out of the earth.

Psalm 104:14

Let us therefore come boldly unto the throne of grace, that we may obtain mercy, and find grace to help in time of need.

Hebrews 4:16

And God is able to make all grace abound toward you; that ye, always having all sufficiency in all things, may abound to every good work.

II Corinthians 9:8

...for your Father knoweth what things ye have need of, before ye ask him.

Matthew 6:8

Humble yourselves therefore under the mighty hand of God, that he may exalt you in due time: Casting all your care upon him; for he careth for you.

I Peter 5:6,7

Additional Scripture References

Gen. 1:29; Ex. 16:11-35; Ps. 34:9; 37:3-5; 46:1; 84:11; 111:5; 113:7,8; Prov. 28:27; Is. 65:24; Luke 6:38; 12:27-31; I Jn. 3:17

Overcoming the World

For whatsoever is born of God overcometh the world: and this is the victory that overcometh the world, even our faith. Who is he that overcometh the world, but he that believeth that Jesus is the Son of God?

I John 5:4,5

Ye are of God, little children, and have overcome them: because greater is he that is in you, than he that is in the world.

I John 4:4

These things I have spoken unto you, that in me ye might have peace. In the world ye shall have tribulation: but be of good cheer; I have overcome the world.

John 16:33

Therefore, my beloved brethren, be ye stedfast, unmoveable, always abounding in the work of the Lord, forasmuch as ye know that your labour is not in vain in the Lord.

I Corinthians 15:58

And ye shall be hated of all men for my name's sake: but he that endureth to the end shall be saved.

Matthew 10:22

Nay, in all these things we are more than conquerors through him that loved us.

Romans 8:37

But thanks be to God, which giveth us the victory through our Lord Jesus Christ.

I Corinthians 15:57

Blessed is the man that endureth temptation: for when he is tried, he shall receive the crown of life, which the Lord hath promised to them that love him.

James 1:12

Be not overcome of evil, but overcome evil with good.

Romans 12:21

He that overcometh shall inherit all things; and I will be his God, and he shall be my son.

Revelation 21:7

Additional Scripture References

II Pet. 1:10,11; 2:19,20; I Jn. 2:13,14; Rev. 2:7; 2:11; 2:17; 2:26; 3:5; 3:12; 3:21; 17:14

Patience

Wherefore seeing we also are compassed about with so great a cloud of witnesses, let us lay aside every weight, and the sin which doth so easily beset us, and let us run with patience the race that is set before us.

Hebrews 12:1

And the servant of the Lord must not strive; but be gentle unto all men, apt to teach, patient, In meekness instructing those that oppose themselves; if God peradventure will give them repentance to the acknowledging of the truth.

II Tim. 2:24,25

My brethren, count it all joy when ye fall into divers temptations; Knowing this, that the trying of your faith worketh patience. But let patience have her perfect work, that ye may be perfect and entire, wanting nothing.

James 1:2-4

For whatsoever things were written aforetime were written for our learning, that we through patience and comfort of the scriptures might have hope.

Romans 15:4

But if we hope for that we see not, then do we with patience wait for it.

Romans 8:25

For ye have need of patience, that, after ye have done the will of God, ye might receive the promise.

Hebrews 10:36

Rest in the Lord, and wait patiently for him: fret not thyself because of him who prospereth in his way, because of the man who bringeth wicked devices to pass.

Psalm 37:7

Be patient therefore, brethren, unto the coming of the Lord. Behold, the husbandman waiteth for the precious fruit of the earth, and hath long patience for it, until he receive the early and latter rain. Be ye also patient; stablish your hearts: for the coming of the Lord draweth nigh.

James 5:7,8

And let us not be weary in well doing: for in due season we shall reap, if we faint not.

Galatians 6:9

Additional Scripture References

Ecc. 7:8; Luke 21:19; Rom. 5:3; 12:9-21; II Cor. 6:1-10; Eph. 4:1,2; Col. 1:9-11; 3:12,13; I Thes. 1:3; II Thes. 3:5; I Tim. 6:11; Titus 2:1,2; Heb. 6:11-15; I Pet. 2:19,20; II Pet. 1:5-7

Peace of God

And the peace of God, which passeth all understanding, shall keep your hearts and minds through Christ Jesus.

Philippians 4:7

Therefore being justified by faith, we have peace with God through our Lord Jesus Christ.

Romans 5:1

These things I have spoken unto you, that in me ye might have peace. In the world ye shall have tribulation: but be of good cheer; I have overcome the world.

John 16:33

For unto us a child is born, unto us a son is given: and the government shall be upon his shoulder: and his name shall be called Wonderful, Counsellor, The mighty God, The everlasting Father, The Prince of Peace.

Isaiah 9:6

For the kingdom of God is not meat and drink; but righteousness, and peace, and joy in the Holy Ghost.

Romans 14:17

For to be carnally minded is death; but to be spiritually minded is life and peace.

Romans 8:6

Take my yoke upon you, and learn of me; for I am meek and lowly in heart: and ye shall find rest unto your souls.

Matthew 11:29

And the work of righteousness shall be peace; and the effect of righteousness quietness and assurance for ever.

Isaiah 32:17

Thou wilt keep him in perfect peace, whose mind is stayed on thee: because he trusteth in thee.

Isaiah 26:3

But the fruit of the Spirit is love, joy, peace, longsuffering, gentleness, goodness, faith.

Galatians 5:22

The Lord will give strength unto his people; the Lord will bless his people with peace.

Psalm 29:11

Mark the perfect man, and behold the upright: for the end of that man is peace.

Psalm 37:37

Additional Scripture References

Job 22:21; Ps. 37:11; 133:1; Prov. 3:13-17; 15:17; 17:1; Is. 11:6; Rom. 10:15; 14:19; 15:13; I Cor. 14:33; II Thes. 3:16; James 3:14-18

Praising God

From the rising of the sun unto the going down of the same the Lord's name is to be praised.

Psalm 113:3

It came even to pass, as the trumpeters and singers were as one, to make one sound to be heard in praising and thanking the Lord; and when they lifted up their voice with the trumpets and cymbals and instruments of musick, and praised the Lord, saying, For he is good; for his mercy endureth for ever: that then the house was filled with a cloud, even the house of the Lord; So that the priests could not stand to minister by reason of the cloud: for the glory of the Lord had filled the house of God.

II Chronicles 5:13,14

Great is the Lord, and greatly to be praised in the city of our God, in the mountain of his holiness.

Psalm 48:1

But thou art holy, O thou that inhabitest the praises of Israel.

Psalm 22:3

The heavens declare the glory of God; and the firmament sheweth his handiwork.

Psalm 19:1

Now I Nebuchadnezzar praise and extol and honour the King of heaven, all whose works are truth, and his ways judgment: and those that walk in pride he is able to abase.

Daniel 4:37

And the heavens shall praise thy wonders, O Lord: thy faithfulness also in the congregation of the saints.

Psalm 89:5

Let every thing that hath breath praise the Lord. Praise ye the Lord.

Psalm 150:6

Whoso offereth praise glorifieth me: and to him that ordereth his conversation aright will I shew the salvation of God.

Psalm 50:23

Oh that men would praise the Lord for his goodness, and for his wonderful works to the children of men!

Psalm 107:8

I will extol thee, my God, O king; and I will bless thy name for ever and ever. Every day will I bless thee; and I will praise thy name for ever and ever. Great is the Lord, and greatly to be praised; and his greatness is unsearchable.

Psalm 145:1-3

Praise ye the Lord. Praise God in his sanctuary: praise him in the firmament of his power. Praise him for his mighty acts: praise him according to his excellent greatness.

Psalm 150:1,2

PRAISING GOD

I am the Lord: that is my name: and my glory will I not give to another, neither my praise to graven images.

Isaiah 42:8

Enter into his gates with thanksgiving, and into his courts with praise: be thankful unto him, and bless his name.

Psalm 100:4

And he hath put a new song in my mouth, even praise unto our God: many shall see it, and fear, and shall trust in the Lord.

Psalm 40:3

I will sing unto the Lord as long as I live: I will sing praise to my God while I have my being.

Psalm 104:33

Moreover four thousand were porters; and four thousand praised the Lord with the instruments which I made, said David, to praise therewith.

I Chronicles 23:5

The Lord is my strength and my shield; my heart trusted in him, and I am helped: therefore my heart greatly rejoiceth; and with my song will I praise him.

Psalm 28:7

In God I will praise his word, in God I have put my trust; I will not fear what flesh can do unto me.

Psalm 56:4

O praise the Lord, all ye nations: praise him, all ye people. For his merciful kindness is great toward us: and the truth of the Lord endureth for ever. Praise ye the Lord.

Psalm 117:1,2

Which is the earnest of our inheritance until the redemption of the purchased possession, unto the praise of his glory.

Ephesians 1:14

Let them praise thy great and terrible name; for it is holy.

Psalm 99:3

My heart is fixed, O God, my heart is fixed: I will sing and give praise.

Psalm 57:7

Therefore judge nothing before the time, until the Lord come, who both will bring to light the hidden things of darkness, and will make manifest the counsels of the hearts: and then shall every man have praise of God.

I Corinthians 4:5

I will also praise thee with the psaltery, even thy truth, O my God: unto thee will I sing with the harp, O thou Holy One of Israel.

Psalm 71:22

Wherefore God also hath highly exalted him, and given him a name which is above every name: That at the name of Jesus every knee should bow, of things in heaven, and things in earth, and things under the earth; And

that every tongue should confess that Jesus Christ is Lord, to the glory of God the Father.
Philippians 2:9-11

Give unto the Lord the glory due unto his name; worship the Lord in the beauty of holiness.
Psalm 29:2

Be glad in the Lord, and rejoice, ye righteous: and shout for joy, all ye that are upright in heart.
Psalm 32:11

Rejoice in the Lord, O ye righteous: for praise is comely for the upright.
Psalm 33:1

I will call on the Lord, who is worthy to be praised: so shall I be saved from mine enemies.
II Samuel 22:4

Praise ye the Lord: for it is good to sing praises unto our God; for it is pleasant; and praise is comely.
Psalm 147:1

And when the chief priests and scribes saw the wonderful things that he did, and the children crying in the temple, and saying, Hosanna to the son of David; they were sore displeased, And said unto him, Hearest thou what these say? And Jesus saith unto them, Yea; have ye never read, Out of the mouth of babes and sucklings thou hast perfected praise?
Matthew 21:15,16

PRAISING GOD

O clap your hands, all ye people; shout unto God with the voice of triumph.

Psalm 47:1

O let not the oppressed return ashamed: let the poor and needy praise thy name.

Psalm 74:21

Finally, brethren, whatsoever things are true, whatsoever things are honest, whatsoever things are just, whatsoever things are pure, whatsoever things are lovely, whatsoever things are of good report; if there be any virtue, and if there by any praise, think on these things.

Philippians 4:8

Let them shout for joy, and be glad, that favour my righteous cause: yea, let them say continually, Let the Lord be magnified, which hath pleasure in the prosperity of his servant.

Psalm 35:27

That the trial of your faith, being much more precious than of gold that perisheth, though it be tried with fire, might be found unto praise and honour and glory at the appearing of Jesus Christ.

I Peter 1:7

And suddenly there was with the angel a multitude of the heavenly host praising God, and saying, Glory to God in the highest, and on earth peace, good will toward men.

Luke 2:13,14

Prayer

After this manner therefore pray ye: Our Father which art in heaven, Hallowed be thy name. Thy kingdom come. Thy will be done in earth, as it is in heaven. Give us this day our daily bread. And forgive us our debts, as we forgive our debtors. And lead us not into temptation, but deliver us from evil: For thine is the kingdom, and the power, and the glory, for ever. Amen.

Matthew 6:9-13

And when he had taken the book, the four beasts and four and twenty elders fell down before the Lamb, having every one of them harps, and golden vials full of odours, which are the prayers of saints.

Revelation 5:8

Confess your faults one to another, and pray one for another, that ye may be healed. The effectual fervent prayer of a righteous man availeth much.

James 5:16

Let us therefore come boldly unto the throne of grace, that we may obtain mercy, and find grace to help in time of need.

Hebrews 4:16

If my people, which are called by my name, shall humble themselves, and pray, and seek my face, and turn from their wicked ways;

then will I hear from heaven, and will forgive their sin, and will heal their land.

II Chronicles 7:14

Rejoice evermore. Pray without ceasing. In every thing give thanks: for this is the will of God in Christ Jesus concerning you.

I Thessalonians 5:16-18

Now we know that God heareth not sinners: but if any man be a worshipper of God, and doeth his will, him he heareth.

John 9:31

The sacrifice of the wicked is an abomination to the Lord: but the prayer of the upright is his delight.

Proverbs 15:8

Evening, and morning, and at noon, will I pray, and cry aloud: and he shall hear my voice.

Psalm 55:17

Additional Scripture References

Num. 11:1,2; Josh. 10:12-14; I Kin. 9:3; II Kin. 20:5; Ps. 65:2; 102:17; Is. 38:5; Matt. 14:23; 17:14-21; 26:36; Mark 11:24; 14:38; Luke 11:9; 18:1; 21:36; Acts 4:31; 6:4; Rom. 8:26; 12:12; I Tim. 2:8; James 1:5,6; 5:13-15

Pride

Every one that is proud in heart is an abomination to the Lord: though hand join in hand, he shall not be unpunished.

Proverbs 16:5

Pride goeth before destruction, and an haughty spirit before a fall. Better it is to be of an humble spirit with the lowly, than to divide the spoil with the proud.

Proverbs 16:18,19

Love not the world, neither the things that are in the world. If any man love the world, the love of the Father is not in him. For all that is in the world, the lust of the flesh, and the lust of the eyes, and the pride of life, is not of the Father, but is of the world.

I John 2:15,16

But he giveth more grace. Wherefore he saith, God resisteth the proud, but giveth grace unto the humble.

James 4:6

And whosoever shall exalt himself shall be abased; and he that shall humble himself shall be exalted.

Matthew 23:12

The wicked, through the pride of his countenance, will not seek after God: God is not in all his thoughts.

Psalm 10:4

Though the Lord be high, yet hath he respect unto the lowly: but the proud he knoweth afar off.

Psalm 138:6

Blessed is that man that maketh the Lord his trust, and respecteth not the proud, nor such as turn aside to lies.

Psalm 40:4

The lofty looks of man shall be humbled, and the haughtiness of men shall be bowed down, and the Lord alone shall be exalted in that day. For the day of the Lord of hosts shall be upon every one that is proud and lofty, and upon every one that is lifted up; and he shall be brought low.

Isaiah 2:11,12

The fear of the Lord is to hate evil: pride, and arrogancy, and the evil way, and the froward mouth, do I hate.

Proverbs 8:13

Additional Scripture References

Deut. 8:11-14; Ps. 49:6-14; 101:5;
Prov. 6:16-19; 15:25; 21:4; 28:25; 29:23;
Is. 13:11; Jer. 9:23,24; 50:31,32; Mal. 4:1;
Mark 7:20-23; Luke 14:8-11; Rom. 1:28-32

The Rapture

For the Lord himself shall descend from heaven with a shout, with the voice of the archangel, and with the trump of God: and the dead in Christ shall rise first: Then we which are alive and remain shall be caught up together with them in the clouds, to meet the Lord in the air: and so shall we ever be with the Lord.

I Thessalonians 4:16,17

Behold, I shew you a mystery; We shall not all sleep, but we shall all be changed, In a moment, in the twinkling of an eye, at the last trump: for the trumpet shall sound, and the dead shall be raised incorruptible, and we shall be changed.

I Corinthians 15:51,52

And to wait for his Son from heaven, whom he raised from the dead, even Jesus, which delivered us from the wrath to come.

I Thessalonians 1:10

Watch ye therefore, and pray always, that ye may be accounted worthy to escape all these things that shall come to pass, and to stand before the Son of man.

Luke 21:36

Then shall two be in the field; the one shall be taken, and the other left. Two women shall be grinding at the mill; the one shall be taken, and the other left. Watch therefore: for ye know not what hour your Lord doth come.

Matthew 24:40-42

Beloved, now are we the sons of God, and it doth not yet appear what we shall be: but we know that, when he shall appear, we shall be like him; for we shall see him as he is.

I John 3:2

Now learn a parable of the fig tree; When his branch is yet tender, and putteth forth leaves, ye know that summer is nigh: So likewise ye, when ye shall see all these things, know that it is near, even at the doors.

Matthew 24:32,33

When Christ, who is our life, shall appear, then shall ye also appear with him in glory.

Colossians 3:4

He which testifieth these things saith, Surely I come quickly. Amen. Even so, come, Lord Jesus.

Revelation 22:20

Additional Scripture References

Matt. 24:37-39; John 14:1-3; Acts 1:9-11; Phil. 3:20,21; I Thes. 5:9; II Thes. 2:1-3; Titus 2:11-13; I Pet. 1:7; II Pet. 3:3,4; Rev. 1:7; 3:11; 22:7

Reconciliation

And one lamb out of the flock, out of two hundred, out of the fat pastures of Israel; for a meat offering, and for a burnt offering, and for peace offerings, to make reconciliation for them, saith the Lord God.

Ezekiel 45:15

Therefore if any man be in Christ, he is a new creature: old things are passed away; behold, all things are become new. And all things are of God, who hath reconciled us to himself by Jesus Christ, and hath given to us the ministry of reconciliation; To wit, that God was in Christ, reconciling the world unto himself, not imputing their trespasses unto them; and hath committed unto us the word of reconciliation.

II Corinthians 5:17-19

For it pleased the Father that in him should all fulness dwell; And, having made peace through the blood of his cross, by him to reconcile all things unto himself; by him, I say, whether they be things in earth, or things in heaven. And you, that were sometime alienated and enemies in your mind by wicked works, yet now hath he reconciled In the body of his flesh through death, to present you holy and unblameable and unreproveable in his sight.

Colossians 1:19-22

But now in Christ Jesus ye who sometimes were far off are made nigh by the blood of Christ. For he is our peace, who hath made both one, and hath broken down the middle wall of partition between us; Having abolished in his flesh the enmity, even the law of commandments contained in ordinances; for to make in himself of twain one new man, so making peace; And that he might reconcile both unto God in one body by the cross, having slain the enmity thereby: And came and preached peace to you which were afar off, and to them that were nigh.

Ephesians 2:13-17

Wherefore in all things it behooved him to be made like unto his brethren, that he might be a merciful and faithful high priest in things pertaining to God, to make reconciliation for the sins of the people.

Hebrews 2:17

Additional Scripture References

Lev. 8:14,15; II Chr. 29:23,24: Rom. 5:10

Redemption

Who gave himself for us, that he might redeem us from all iniquity, and purify unto himself a peculiar people, zealous of good works.

Titus 2:14

Who hath delivered us from the power of darkness, and hath translated us into the kingdom of his dear Son: In whom we have redemption through his blood, even the forgiveness of sins.

Colossians 1:13,14

For there is one God, and one mediator between God and men, the man Christ Jesus; Who gave himself a ransom for all, to be testified in due time.

I Timothy 2:5,6

Forasmuch as ye know that ye were not redeemed with corruptible things, as silver and gold, from your vain conversation received by tradition from your fathers; But with the precious blood of Christ, as of a lamb without blemish and without spot.

I Peter 1:18,19

For all have sinned, and come short of the glory of God; Being justified freely by his grace through the redemption that is in Christ Jesus.

Romans 3:23,24

For he hath made him to be sin for us, who knew no sin; that we might be made the righteousness of God in him.

II Corinthians 5:21

In whom we have redemption through his blood, the forgiveness of sins, according to the riches of his grace.

Ephesians 1:7

But when the fulness of the time was come, God sent forth his Son, made of a woman, made under the law, To redeem them that were under the law, that we might receive the adoption of sons.

Galatians 4:4,5

Neither by the blood of goats and calves, but by his own blood he entered in once into the holy place, having obtained eternal redemption for us.

Hebrews 9:12

Additional Scripture References

Ps. 34:22; 103:1-5; Is. 49:26; Matt. 20:27,28; Luke 1:68-75; I Cor. 1:30; Gal. 1:3,4; Titus 2:11-14; Heb. 9:1-28; Rev. 5:9

Rejoicing in the Lord

Therefore being justified by faith, we have peace with God through our Lord Jesus Christ: By whom also we have access by faith into this grace wherein we stand, and rejoice in hope of the glory of God.

Romans 5:1,2

And Hannah prayed, and said, My heart rejoiceth in the Lord, mine horn is exalted in the Lord: my mouth is enlarged over mine enemies; because I rejoice in thy salvation.

I Samuel 2:1

Rejoice in the Lord alway: and again I say, Rejoice.

Philippians 4:4

I will greatly rejoice in the Lord, my soul shall be joyful in my God; for he hath clothed me with the garments of salvation, he hath covered me with the robe of righteousness, as a bridegroom decketh himself with ornaments, and as a bride adorneth herself with her jewels.

Isaiah 61:10

Rejoice evermore.

I Thessalonians 5:16

... and ye shall rejoice before the Lord your God seven days.

Leviticus 23:40

For ye shall go out with joy, and be led forth with peace: the mountains and the hills shall break forth before you into singing, and all the trees of the field shall clap their hands.

Isaiah 55:12

Be glad in the Lord, and rejoice, ye righteous: and shout for joy, all ye that are upright in heart.

Psalm 32:11

And it shall be said in that day, Lo, this is our God; we have waited for him, and he will save us: this is the Lord; we have waited for him, we will be glad and rejoice in his salvation.

Isaiah 25:9

But let all those that put their trust in thee rejoice: let them ever shout for joy, because thou defendest them: let them also that love thy name be joyful in thee.

Psalm 5:11

Additional Scripture References

Deut. 12:7; 26:11; I Chr. 16:10; Ps. 20:5; 33:1; 65:8-13; 96:11-13; Prov. 24:17; 28:12; Is. 14:7,8; 35:1,2; 41:10-20; Hab. 3:18; Zeph. 3:14; Zech. 2:10; 9:9; Matt. 5:11,12; Luke 6:22,23; Acts 5:41; I Pet. 4:13

Renewing Your Mind

And be not conformed to this world: but be ye transformed by the renewing of your mind, that ye may prove what is that good, and acceptable, and perfect, will of God.

Romans 12:2

But put ye on the Lord Jesus Christ, and make not provision for the flesh, to fulfil the lusts thereof.

Romans 13:14

Create in me a clean heart, O God; and renew a right spirit within me.

Psalm 51:10

Cast away from you all your transgressions, whereby ye have transgressed; and make you a new heart and a new spirit: for why will ye die, O house of Israel?

Ezekiel 18:31

A new heart also will I give you, and a new spirit will I put within you: and I will take away the stony heart out of your flesh, and I will give you an heart of flesh.

Ezekiel 36:26

Therefore if any man be in Christ, he is a new creature: old things are passed away; behold, all things are become new.

II Corinthians 5:17

And be renewed in the spirit of your mind.

Ephesians 4:23

And you, that were sometime alienated and enemies in your mind by wicked works, yet now hath he reconciled.

Colossians 1:21

For which cause we faint not; but though our outward man perish, yet the inward man is renewed day by day.

II Corinthians 4:16

Additional Scripture References

Is. 43:18,19; Gal. 5:16-25; 6:15; Eph. 4:1; Col. 3:8-17

Repentance

From that time Jesus began to preach, and to say, Repent: for the kingdom of heaven is at hand.

Matthew 4:17

Now after that John was put in prison, Jesus came into Galilee, preaching the gospel of the kingdom of God, And saying, The time is fulfilled, and the kingdom of God is at hand: repent ye, and believe the gospel.

Mark 1:14,15

And the times of this ignorance God winked at; but now commandeth all men everywhere to repent.

Acts 17:30

Then began he to upbraid the cities wherein most of his mighty works were done, because they repented not.

Matthew 11:20

Cast away from you all your transgressions, whereby ye have transgressed; and make you a new heart and a new spirit: for why will ye die, O house of Israel?

Ezekiel 18:31

I say unto you, that likewise joy shall be in heaven over one sinner that repenteth, more than over ninety and nine just persons, which need no repentance.

Luke 15:7

Or despisest thou the riches of his goodness and forbearance and longsuffering; not knowing that the goodness of God leadeth thee to repentance?

Romans 2:4

But go ye and learn what that meaneth, I will have mercy, and not sacrifice: for I am not come to call the righteous, but sinners to repentance.

Matthew 9:13

Repent ye therefore, and be converted, that your sins may be blotted out, when the times of refreshing shall come from the presence of the Lord.

Acts 3:19

I tell you, Nay: but, except ye repent, ye shall all likewise perish.

Luke 13:3

Additional Scripture References

Ps. 119:59; Mark 6:12; Luke 3:3; 24:47; Acts 2:38; II Cor. 7:9,10; II Tim. 2:24-26

Righteousness

Righteousness exalteth a nation: but sin is a reproach to any people.

Proverbs 14:34

Blessed are they which do hunger and thirst after righteousness: for they shall be filled.

Matthew 5:6

For the kingdom of God is not meat and drink; but righteousness, and peace, and joy in the Holy Ghost.

Romans 14:17

And they that be wise shall shine as the brightness of the firmament; and they that turn many to righteousness as the stars for ever and ever.

Daniel 12:3

For the righteous Lord loveth righteousness; his countenance doth behold the upright.

Psalm 11:7

But seek ye first the kingdom of God, and his righteousness; and all these things shall be added unto you.

Matthew 6:33

And be renewed in the spirit of your mind; And that ye put on the new man, which after God is created in righteousness and true holiness.

Ephesians 4:23,24

For I say unto you, That except your righteousness shall exceed the righteousness of the scribes and Pharisees, ye shall in no case enter into the kingdom of heaven.

Matthew 5:20

Let not sin therefore reign in your mortal body, that ye should obey it in the lusts thereof. Neither yield ye your members as instruments of unrighteousness unto sin: but yield yourselves unto God, as those that are alive from the dead, and your members as instruments of righteousness unto God.

Romans 6:12,13

Then shall the righteous shine forth as the sun in the kingdom of their Father. Who hath ears to hear, let him hear.

Matthew 13:43

Additional Scripture References

Ps. 15:1,2; 33:4,5; 97:6; 125:1-3; Prov. 10:2; Is. 61:10; Hos. 10:12; Mal. 3:16-18; Matt. 5:10; 12:35; Rom. 1:16,17; 4:1-8; 4:13; II Cor. 5:21; Eph. 6:14; Phil. 3:7-9; I Tim. 6:11; II Tim. 2:22; Heb. 12:11; I Jn. 2:29; 3:7

Salvation

I call heaven and earth to record this day against you, that I have set before you life and death, blessing and cursing: therefore choose life, that both thou and thy seed may live.

Deuteronomy 30:19

For God so loved the world, that he gave his only begotten Son, that whosoever believeth in him should not perish, but have everlasting life. For God sent not his Son into the world to condemn the world; but that the world through him might be saved.

John 3:16,17

For by grace are ye saved through faith; and that not of yourselves: it is the gift of God: Not of works, lest any man should boast.

Ephesians 2:8,9

That if thou shalt confess with thy mouth the Lord Jesus, and shalt believe in thine heart that God hath raised him from the dead, thou shalt be saved. For with the heart man believeth unto righteousness; and with the mouth confession is made unto salvation.

Romans 10:9,10

But if we walk in the light, as he is in the light, we have fellowship one with another, and the blood of Jesus Christ his Son cleanseth us from all sin.

I John 1:7

And they said, Believe on the Lord Jesus Christ, and thou shalt be saved, and thy house.

Acts 16:31

Jesus answered and said unto him, Verily, verily, I say unto thee, Except a man be born again, he cannot see the kingdom of God.

John 3:3

Jesus saith unto him, I am the way, the truth, and the life: no man cometh unto the Father, but by me.

John 14:6

Verily, verily, I say unto you, He that believeth on me hath everlasting life.

John 6:47

Verily, verily, I say unto you, He that heareth my word, and believeth on him that sent me, hath everlasting life, and shall not come into condemnation; but is passed from death unto life.

John 5:24

Additional Scripture References

Ps. 25:5; 50:23; Is. 12:2; 45:22; 51:8; Matt. 18:3; 18:11; John 3:36; 4:14; 10:9; Acts 2:21; 4:12; Rom. 1:16; 5:8; I Thes. 5:9; II Tim. 2:10; Titus 2:11; Heb. 7:25; I Pet. 1:7-10

Sanctification

And such were some of you: but ye are washed, but ye are sanctified, but ye are justified in the name of the Lord Jesus, and by the Spirit of our God.

I Corinthians 6:11

And now, brethren, I commend you to God, and to the word of his grace, which is able to build you up, and to give you an inheritance among all them which are sanctified.

Acts 20:32

That we henceforth be no more children, tossed to and fro, and carried about with every wind of doctrine, by the sleight of men, and cunning craftiness, whereby they lie in wait to deceive; But speaking the truth in love, may grow up into him in all things, which is the head, even Christ.

Ephesians 4:14,15

Being confident of this very thing, that he which hath begun a good work in you will perform it until the day of Jesus Christ.

Philippians 1:6

How much more shall the blood of Christ, who through the eternal Spirit offered himself without spot to God, purge your conscience from dead works to serve the living God?

Hebrews 9:14

For it became him, for whom are all things, and by whom are all things, in bringing many sons unto glory, to make the captain of their salvation perfect through sufferings. For both he that sanctifieth and they who are sanctified are all of one: for which cause he is not ashamed to call them brethren.

Hebrews 2:10,11

But we are bound to give thanks alway to God for you, brethren beloved of the Lord, because God hath from the beginning chosen you to salvation through sanctification of the Spirit and belief of the truth.

II Thessalonians 2:13

Thou shalt sanctify him therefore; for he offereth the bread of thy God: he shall be holy unto thee: for I the Lord, which sanctify you, am holy.

Leviticus 21:8

Additional Scripture References

Ezek. 20:12; John 17:14-23; Acts 15:8,9; Rom. 8:9,10; I Cor. 1:30; 7:14; Eph. 5:25-27; I Thes. 5:23; II Tim. 2:21; Heb. 13:12; I Pet. 1:2; 1:22; II Pet. 3:18; Jude 1

Satan

And he said unto them, I beheld Satan as lightning fall from heaven.

Luke 10:18

And the great dragon was cast out, that old serpent, called the Devil, and Satan, which deceiveth the whole world: he was cast out into the earth, and his angels were cast out with him.

Revelation 12:9

Be sober, be vigilant; because your adversary the devil, as a roaring lion, walketh about, seeking whom he may devour.

I Peter 5:8

Ye are of your father the devil, and the lusts of your father ye will do. He was a murderer from the beginning, and abode not in the truth, because there is no truth in him. When he speaketh a lie, he speaketh of his own: for he is a liar, and the father of it.

John 8:44

Put on the whole armour of God, that ye may be able to stand against the wiles of the devil. For we wrestle not against flesh and blood, but against principalities, against powers, against the rulers of the darkness of this world, against spiritual wickedness in high places.

Ephesians 6:11,12

But if our gospel be hid, it is hid to them that are lost: In whom the god of this world hath blinded the minds of them which believe not, lest the light of the glorious gospel of Christ, who is the image of God, should shine unto them.

II Corinthians 4:3,4

He that committeth sin is of the devil; for the devil sinneth from the beginning. For this purpose the Son of God was manifested, that he might destroy the works of the devil.

I John 3:8

And no marvel; for Satan himself is transformed into an angel of light.

II Corinthians 11:14

. . . and which have not known the depths of Satan, . . .

Revelation 2:24

Additional Scripture References

Gen. 3:1-5; Is. 14:12-20; Ezek. 28:12-19; Zech. 3:1; Matt. 4:1-11; 16:23; 25:41; Mark 4:15; John 13:2; 14:30; II Cor. 2:11; Eph. 2:1,2; I Thes. 3:5; Heb. 2:14; I Jn. 3:10; Rev. 12:2-10

Satan Defeated

And having spoiled principalities and powers, he made a shew of them openly, triumphing over them in it.

Colossians 2:15

And I will put enmity between thee and the woman, and between thy seed and her seed; it shall bruise thy head, and thou shalt bruise his heel.

Genesis 3:15

Therefore will I divide him a portion with the great, and he shall divide the spoil with the strong; because he hath poured out his soul unto death: and he was numbered with the transgressors; and he bare the sin of many, and made intercession for the transgressors.

Isaiah 53:12

Behold, I give unto you power to tread on serpents and scorpions, and over all the power of the enemy: and nothing shall by any means hurt you.

Luke 10:19

Now is the judgment of this world: now shall the prince of this world be cast out.

John 12:31

Forasmuch then as the children are partakers of flesh and blood, he also himself likewise took part of the same; that through death he might destroy him that had the power

of death, that is, the devil.
Hebrews 2:14

Wherefore he saith, When he ascended up on high, he led captivity captive, and gave gifts unto men.
Ephesians 4:8

Remember that Jesus Christ of the seed of David was raised from the dead according to my gospel.
II Timothy 2:8

He that committeth sin is of the devil; for the devil sinneth from the beginning. For this purpose the Son of God was manifested, that he might destroy the works of the devil.
I John 3:8

And the devil that deceived them was cast into the lake of fire and brimstone, where the beast and the false prophet are, and shall be tormented day and night for ever and ever.
Revelation 20:10

Additional Scripture References

Ps. 44:5; Is. 14:12-20; Mal. 4:3;
Matt. 4:1-11;16:18,19; Luke 4:13;
John 14:30; 16:33; I Jn. 2:14; 4:4; 5:4;
Rev. 12:11; 15:2

Seeking God

But seek ye first the kingdom of God, and his righteousness; and all these things shall be added unto you.

Matthew 6:33

For I know the thoughts that I think toward you, saith the Lord, thoughts of peace, and not of evil, to give you an expected end. Then shall ye call upon me, and ye shall go and pray unto me, and I will hearken unto you. And ye shall seek me, and find me, when ye shall search for me with all your heart.

Jeremiah 29:11-13

Submit yourselves therefore to God. Resist the devil, and he will flee from you. Draw nigh to God, and he will draw nigh to you. Cleanse your hands, ye sinners; and purify your hearts, ye double minded.

James 4:7,8

Woe to them that go down to Egypt for help; and stay on horses, and trust in chariots, because they are many; and in horsemen, because they are very strong; but they look not unto the Holy One of Israel, neither seek the Lord!

Isaiah 31:1

But without faith it is impossible to please him: for he that cometh to God must believe that he is, and that he is a rewarder of them that diligently seek him.

Hebrews 11:6

Glory ye in his holy name: let the heart of them rejoice that seek the Lord. Seek the Lord, and his strength: seek his face evermore. Remember his marvellous works that he hath done; his wonders, and the judgments of his mouth.

Psalm 105:3-5

And they that know thy name will put their trust in thee: for thou, Lord, hast not forsaken them that seek thee.

Psalm 9:10

I have not spoken in secret, in a dark place of the earth: I said not unto the seed of Jacob, Seek ye me in vain: I the Lord speak righteousness, I declare things that are right.

Isaiah 45:19

The Lord is good unto them that wait for him, to the soul that seeketh him.

Lamentations 3:25

Additional Scripture References

Deut. 4:29-31; II Chr. 15:1,2; 15:12-15; Ps. 10:4; 22:26; 34:4; 34:10; 69:30-33; 70:4; 83:16; 119:2; Prov. 1:23-33; Is. 55:6; Hosea 10:12; Zeph. 1:4-6; 2:3

Self Denial

And he said to them all, If any man will come after me, let him deny himself, and take up his cross daily, and follow me.

Luke 9:23

For the grace of God that bringeth salvation hath appeared to all men, Teaching us that, denying ungodliness and worldly lusts, we should live soberly, righteously, and godly, in this present world.

Titus 2:11,12

And they overcame him by the blood of the Lamb, and by the word of their testimony; and they loved not their lives unto the death.

Revelation 12:11

Yea doubtless, and I count all things but loss for the excellency of the knowledge of Christ Jesus my Lord: for whom I have suffered the loss of all things, and do count them but dung, that I may win Christ.

Philippians 3:8

Wherefore, if meat make my brother to offend, I will eat no flesh while the world standeth, lest I make my brother to offend.

I Corinthians 8:13

And when they had brought their ships to land, they forsook all, and followed him.

Luke 5:11

Again, the kingdom of heaven is like

unto a merchant man, seeking goodly pearls:
Who, when he had found one pearl of great
price, went and sold all that he had, and bought
it.

Matthew 13:45,46

So likewise, whosoever he be of you
that forsaketh not all that he hath, he cannot be
my disciple.

Luke 14:33

But I keep under my body, and bring it
into subjection: lest that by any means, when I
have preached to others, I myself should be a
castaway.

I Corinthians 9:27

And he said unto them, Verily I say
unto you, There is no man that hath left house,
or parents, or brethren, or wife, or children, for
the kingdom of God's sake, Who shall not
receive manifold more in this present time, and
in the world to come life everlasting.

Luke 18:29,30

Additional Scripture References

Matt. 4:18-20; 18:8; 19:21; Mark 1:18;
12:41-44; Luke 14:27; Rom. 8:13; I Cor. 9:19;
Gal. 5:16,17; Phil. 2:4-8; Col. 3:5-10;
II Tim. 2:4; I Pet. 2:11-16; 4:1,2

Servanthood

Let this mind be in you, which was also in Christ Jesus: Who, being in the form of God, thought it not robbery to be equal with God: But made himself of no reputation, and took upon him the form of a servant, and was made in the likeness of men.

Philippians 2:5-7

And whosoever will be chief among you, let him be your servant.

Matthew 20:27

For God is not unrighteous to forget your work and labour of love, which ye have shewed toward his name, in that ye have ministered to the saints, and do minister.

Hebrews 6:10

And he sat down, and called the twelve, and saith unto them, If any man desire to be first, the same shall be last of all, and servant of all.

Mark 9:35

For, brethren, ye have been called unto liberty; only use not liberty for an occasion to the flesh, but by love serve one another. For all the law is fulfilled in one word, even in this; Thou shalt love thy neighbour as thyself.

Galatians 5:13,14

For whosoever shall give you a cup of water to drink in my name, because ye belong to

Christ, verily I say unto you, he shall not lose his reward.

Mark 9:41

And the King shall answer and say unto them, Verily I say unto you, Inasmuch as ye have done it unto one of the least of these my brethren, ye have done it unto me.

Matthew 25:40

If I then, your Lord and Master, have washed your feet; ye also ought to wash one another's feet. For I have given you an example, that ye should do as I have done to you.

John 13:14,15

For though I be free from all men, yet have I made myself servant unto all, that I might gain the more.

I Corinthians 9:19

For whether is greater, he that sitteth at meat, or he that serveth? is not he that sitteth at meat? but I am among you as he that serveth.

Luke 22:27

Sin

And when the woman saw that the tree was good for food, and that it was pleasant to the eyes, and a tree to be desired to make one wise, she took of the fruit thereof, and did eat, and gave also unto her husband with her; and he did eat.

Genesis 3:6

For all have sinned, and come short of the glory of God.

Romans 3:23

For the wages of sin is death; but the gift of God is eternal life through Jesus Christ our Lord.

Romans 6:23

Then when lust hath conceived, it bringeth forth sin: and sin, when it is finished, bringeth forth death.

James 1:15

For thou art not a God that hath pleasure in wickedness: neither shall evil dwell with thee. The foolish shall not stand in thy sight: thou hatest all workers of iniquity.

Psalm 5:4,5

Jesus answered them, Verily, verily, I say unto you, Whosoever committeth sin is the servant of sin.

John 8:34

Behold, the Lord's hand is not shortened, that it cannot save; neither his ear heavy, that it cannot hear: But your iniquities have separated between you and your God, and your sins have hid his face from you, that he will not hear.

Isaiah 59:1,2

If we say that we have no sin, we deceive ourselves, and the truth is not in us.

I John 1:8

Righteousness exalteth a nation: but sin is a reproach to any people.

Proverbs 14:34

Therefore to him that knoweth to do good, and doeth it not, to him it is sin.

James 4:17

Additional Scripture References

Gen. 3:1-20; 6:5,6; Ex. 32:33; Num. 32:23; Deut. 25:16; II Chr. 24:20; Ps. 11:5-7; 44:20,21; 66:18; 69:5; Prov. 5:22,23; 8:36; 11:5-7; 11:19,20; Ecc. 12:14; Rom. 5:12-19; 6:1-23; 8:3; Eph. 2:1,2; Heb. 11:24,25; I Jn. 3:8

Spiritual Birth

Whosoever believeth that Jesus is the Christ is born of God: and every one that loveth him that begat loveth him also that is begotten of him.

I John 5:1

But as many as received him, to them gave he power to become the sons of God, even to them that believe on his name: Which were born, not of blood, nor of the will of the flesh, nor of the will of man, but of God.

John 1:12,13

Therefore if any man be in Christ, he is a new creature: old things are passed away; behold, all things are become new.

II Corinthians 5:17

Of his own will begat he us with the word of truth, that we should be a kind of firstfruits of his creatures.

James 1:18

Blessed be the God and Father of our Lord Jesus Christ, which according to his abundant mercy hath begotten us again unto a lively hope by the resurrection of Jesus Christ from the dead.

I Peter 1:3

But we all, with open face beholding as in a glass the glory of the Lord, are changed into the same image from glory to glory, even as by the Spirit of the Lord.

II Corinthians 3:18

A new heart also will I give you, and a new spirit will I put within you: and I will take away the stony heart out of your flesh, and I will give you an heart of flesh.

Ezekiel 36:26

And this is the record, that God hath given to us eternal life, and this life is in his Son. He that hath the Son hath life; and he that hath not the Son of God hath not life.

I John 5:11,12

Being born again, not of corruptible seed, but of incorruptible, by the word of God, which liveth and abideth for ever.

I Peter 1:23

Not by works of righteousness which we have done, but according to his mercy he saved us, by the washing of regeneration, and renewing of the Holy Ghost.

Titus 3:5

Additional Scripture References

Ezek. 11:19; John. 3:1-8; 20:31; Rom. 6:4; 8:1-13; 8:29; Gal. 6:15; Eph. 2:10; 4:17-24; Col. 3:9,10; I Pet. 2:2; II Pet. 1:4; I Jn. 2:29; 4:7

Spiritual Blindness

But if our gospel be hid, it is hid to them that are lost: In whom the god of this world hath blinded the minds of them which believe not, lest the light of the glorious gospel of Christ, who is the image of God, should shine unto them.

II Corinthians 4:3,4

He hath blinded their eyes, and hardened their heart; that they should not see with their eyes, nor understand with their heart, and be converted, and I should heal them.

John 12:40

Then spake Jesus again unto them, saying, I am the light of the world: he that followeth me shall not walk in darkness, but shall have the light of life.

John 8:12

For verily I say unto you, That many prophets and righteous men have desired to see those things which ye see, and have not seen them; and to hear those things which ye hear, and have not heard them.

Matthew 13:17

For we wrestle not against flesh and blood, but against principalities, against powers, against the rulers of the darkness of this world, against spiritual wickedness in high places.

Ephesians 6:12

Hear now this, O foolish people, and without understanding; which have eyes, and see not; which have ears, and hear not.

Jeremiah 5:21

For God, who commanded the light to shine out of darkness, hath shined in our hearts, to give the light of the knowledge of the glory of God in the face of Jesus Christ.

II Corinthians 4:6

But ye are a chosen generation, a royal priesthood, an holy nation, a peculiar people; that ye should shew forth the praises of him who hath called you out of darkness into his marvellous light.

I Peter 2:9

I am come a light into the world, that whosoever believeth on me should not abide in darkness.

John 12:46

Additional Scripture References

Job 5:13,14; Is. 6:9; 59:9,10; Ezek. 12:1,2; Matt. 4:16; 13:1-23; 16:2,3; John 12:35,36; 14:16,17; Acts 26:15-18; Rom. 1:16-21; 13:12; II Cor. 3:12-18; Eph. 4:17-24; 5:8; I Jn. 2:9-11

Suffering - Persecution

And lest I should be exalted above measure through the abundance of the revelations, there was given to me a thorn in the flesh, the messenger of Satan to buffet me, lest I should be exalted above measure. For this thing I besought the Lord thrice, that it might depart from me. And he said unto me, My grace is sufficient for thee: for my strength is made perfect in weakness. Most gladly therefore will I rather glory in my infirmities, that the power of Christ may rest upon me. Therefore I take pleasure in infirmities, in reproaches, in necessities, in persecutions, in distresses for Christ's sake: for when I am weak, then am I strong.

II Corinthians 12:7-10

Blessed be God, even the Father of our Lord Jesus Christ, the Father of mercies, and the God of all comfort; Who comforteth us in all our tribulation, that we may be able to comfort them which are in any trouble, by the comfort wherewith we ourselves are comforted of God.

II Corinthians 1:3,4

These things I have spoken unto you, that in me ye might have peace. In the world ye shall have tribulation: but be of good cheer; I have overcome the world.

John 16:33

Many are the afflictions of the right-eous: but the Lord delivereth him out of them all.

Psalm 34:19

For I reckon that the sufferings of this present time are not worthy to be compared with the glory which shall be revealed in us.

Romans 8:18

Yet if any man suffer as a Christian, let him not be ashamed; but let him glorify God on this behalf.

I Peter 4:16

But as it is written, Eye hath not seen, nor ear heard, neither have entered into the heart of man, the things which God hath pre-pared for them that love him.

I Corinthians 2:9

Thou therefore endure hardness, as a good soldier of Jesus Christ.

II Timothy 2:3

Additional Scripture References

Ps. 11:2; Matt. 5:11,12; Luke 6:22,23; Rom. 5:3-5; 8:28; 8:35-39; 12:14; I Cor. 10:13; II Cor. 4:8-18; 6:1-10; Phil. 1:29; 3:7-11; I Tim. 4:10; II Tim. 3:12; I Pet. 1:6,7; 2:20-25; 3:13-17; 4:14; 5:6-11; Rev. 2:8-11

Temptation

Blessed is the man that endureth temptation: for when he is tried, he shall receive the crown of life, which the Lord hath promised to them that love him. Let no man say when he is tempted, I am tempted of God: for God cannot be tempted with evil, neither tempteth he any man: But every man is tempted, when he is drawn away of his own lust, and enticed.

James 1:12-14

Let us not therefore judge one another any more: but judge this rather, that no man put a stumblingblock or an occasion to fall in his brother's way.

Romans 14:13

Put on the whole armour of God, that ye may be able to stand against the wiles of the devil.

Ephesians 6:11

My son, if sinners entice thee, consent thou not.

Proverbs 1:10

Be sober, be vigilant; because your adversary the devil, as a roaring lion, walketh about, seeking whom he may devour: Whom resist stedfast in the faith, knowing that the same afflictions are accomplished in your brethren that are in the world.

I Peter 5:8,9

Submit yourselves therefore to God. Resist the devil, and he will flee from you.

James 4:7

But I fear, lest by any means, as the serpent beguiled Eve through his subtlety, so your minds should be corrupted from the simplicity that is in Christ.

II Corinthians 11:3

There hath no temptation taken you but such as is common to man: but God is faithful, who will not suffer you to be tempted above that ye are able; but will with the temptation also make a way to escape, that ye may be able to bear it.

I Corinthians 10:13

For in that he himself hath suffered being tempted, he is able to succour them that are tempted.

Hebrews 2:18

Additional Scripture References

Prov. 1:10-18; 7:1-27; 14:27; Matt. 26:40,41; Luke 8:4-13; 17:1; Heb. 4:15; 12:3,4; James 1:2,3; II Pet. 2:9; 3:17; I Jn. 4:4; Rev. 3:10-12

Thankfulness to God

In every thing give thanks: for this is the will of God in Christ Jesus concerning you.

I Thessalonians 5:18

As ye have therefore received Christ Jesus the Lord, so walk ye in him: Rooted and built up in him, and stablished in the faith, as ye have been taught, abounding therein with thanksgiving.

Colossians 2:6,7

And whatsoever ye do in word or deed, do all in the name of the Lord Jesus, giving thanks to God and the Father by him.

Colossians 3:17

By him therefore let us offer the sacrifice of praise to God continually, that is, the fruit of our lips giving thanks to his name. But to do good and to communicate forget not: for with such sacrifices God is well pleased.

Hebrews 13:15,16

Oh that men would praise the Lord for his goodness, and for his wonderful works to the children of men! And let them sacrifice the sacrifices of thanksgiving , and declare his works with rejoicing.

Psalm 107:21,22

O give thanks unto the Lord, for he is good: for his mercy endureth for ever. Let the redeemed of the Lord say so, whom he hath redeemed from the hand of the enemy.

Psalm 107:1,2

Now when Daniel knew that the writing was signed, he went into his house; and his windows being open in his chamber toward Jerusalem, he kneeled upon his knees three times a day, and prayed, and gave thanks before his God, as he did aforetime.

Daniel 6:10

Honour the Lord with thy substance, and with the firstfruits of all thine increase: So shall thy barns be filled with plenty, and thy presses shall burst out with new wine.

Proverbs 3:9,10

For this cause also thank we God without ceasing, because, when ye received the word of God which ye heard of us, ye received it not as the word of men, but as it is in truth, the word of God, which effectually worketh also in you that believe.

I Thessalonians 2:13

Additional Scripture References

I Chr. 23:24-30; 25:1-3; II Chr. 9:8-15; Neh. 12:27-43; Ps. 30:4; 69:30; 92:1; 100:1-5; John 6:11; Acts 2:46,47; 27:33-35; Eph. 5:1-4; 5:15-20; Phil. 4:6; Col. 3:15; I Tim. 2:1

Tithing

Honour the Lord with thy substance, and with the firstfruits of all thine increase: So shall thy barns be filled with plenty, and thy presses shall burst out with new wine.

Proverbs 3:9,10

Will a man rob God? Yet ye have robbed me. But ye say, Wherein have we robbed thee? In tithes and offerings.

Malachi 3:8

Bring ye all the tithes into the storehouse, that there may be meat in mine house, and prove me now herewith, saith the Lord of hosts, if I will not open you the windows of heaven, and pour you out a blessing, that there shall not be room enough to receive it.

Malachi 3:10

The first of the firstfruits of thy land thou shalt bring into the house of the Lord thy God.

Exodus 23:19

And all the tithe of the land, whether of the seed of the land, or of the fruit of the tree, is the Lord's: it is holy unto the Lord.

Leviticus 27:30

And this stone, which I have set for a pillar, shall be God's house: and of all that thou shalt give me I will surely give the tenth unto thee.

Genesis 28:22

And thither ye shall bring your burnt offerings, and your sacrifices, and your tithes, and heave offerings of your hand, and your vows, and your freewill offerings, and the firstlings of your herds and of your flocks.

Deuteronomy 12:6

Thou shalt truly tithe all the increase of thy seed, that the field bringeth forth year by year.

Deuteronomy 14:22

Additional Scripture References

Gen. 14:20; Lev. 27:31-33; Num. 18:12; Deut. 26:1-4; 26:12,13; Neh. 10:35-37; 12:44; 13:5; Amos 4:4; Luke 18:12; Heb. 7:4-6

Tongue - Mouth - Lips

Let the words of my mouth, and the meditation of my heart, be acceptable in thy sight, O Lord, my strength, and my redeemer.

Psalm 19:14

Let no corrupt communication proceed out of your mouth, but that which is good to the use of edifying, that it may minister grace unto the hearers.

Ephesians 4:29

Even so the tongue is a little member, and boasteth great things. Behold, how great a matter a little fire kindleth!

James 3:5

But the tongue can no man tame; it is an unruly evil, full of deadly poison.

James 3:8

The mouth of the just bringeth forth wisdom: but the froward tongue shall be cut out. The lips of the righteous know what is acceptable: but the mouth of the wicked speaketh frowardness.

Proverbs 10:31,32

But I say unto you, That every idle word that men shall speak, they shall give account thereof in the day of judgment. For by thy words thou shalt be justified, and by thy words thou shalt be condemned.

Matthew 12:36,37

A man hath joy by the answer of his mouth: and a word spoken in due season, how good is it!

Proverbs 15:23

Set a watch, O Lord, before my mouth; keep the door of my lips.

Psalm 141:3

Not that which goeth into the mouth defileth a man; but that which cometh out of the mouth, this defileth a man.

Matthew 15:11

Whoso keepeth his mouth and his tongue keepeth his soul from troubles.

Proverbs 21:23

Additional Scripture References

Ps. 10:4,7; 12:3,4; 15:1-3; 34:13; 50:16-23; 52:1-9; 64:1-10; 120:2; Prov. 6:1,2; 10:11; 10:20; 12:17-19; 13:3; 14:3; 15:4; 17:20; 18:7; 18:21; 25:15; 27:2; Ecc. 5:1-5; James 3:1-18; I Pet. 3:10

Trusting God

Thou wilt keep him in perfect peace, whose mind is stayed on thee: because he trusteth in thee. Trust ye in the Lord for ever: for in the Lord JEHOVAH is everlasting strength.

Isaiah 26:3,4

Trust in the Lord with all thine heart; and lean not unto thine own understanding. In all thy ways acknowledge him, and he shall direct thy paths.

Proverbs 3:5,6

As for God, his way is perfect; the word of the Lord is tried: he is a buckler to all them that trust in him.

II Samuel 22:31

The angel of the Lord encampeth round about them that fear him, and delivereth them. O taste and see that the Lord is good: blessed is the man that trusteth in him.

Psalm 34:7,8

The Lord redeemeth the soul of his servants: and none of them that trust in him shall be desolate.

Psalm 34:22

The Lord is good, a strong hold in the day of trouble; and he knoweth them that trust in him.

Nahum 1:7

Oh how great is thy goodness, which thou hast laid up for them that fear thee; which thou hast wrought for them that trust in thee before the sons of men! Thou shalt hide them in the secret of thy presence from the pride of man: thou shalt keep them secretly in a pavilion from the strife of tongues.

Psalm 31:19,20

Trust in the Lord, and do good; so shalt thou dwell in the land, and verily thou shalt be fed. Delight thyself also in the Lord; and he shall give thee the desires of thine heart. Commit thy way unto the Lord; trust also in him; and he shall bring it to pass.

Psalm 37:3-5

It is better to trust in the Lord than to put confidence in man. It is better to trust in the Lord than to put confidence in princes.

Psalm 118:8,9

Additional Scripture References

I Chr. 5:18-20; Job 13:15; Ps. 5:11; 20:7,8; 22:3,4; 28:7; 33:20,21; 37:40; 84:11,12; Prov. 16:20; 22:17-19; Is. 42:17; Jer. 17:5-8; 39:17,18

Truth

Jesus saith unto him, I am the way, the truth, and the life: no man cometh unto the Father, but by me.

John 14:6

Sanctify them through thy truth: thy word is truth.

John 17:17

Buy the truth, and sell it not; also wisdom, and instruction, and understanding.

Proverbs 23:23

For the Lord is good; his mercy is everlasting; and his truth endureth to all generations.

Psalm 100:5

And ye shall know the truth, and the truth shall make you free.

John 8:32

He shall cover thee with his feathers, and under his wings shalt thou trust: his truth shall be thy shield and buckler.

Psalm 91:4

By mercy and truth iniquity is purged: and by the fear of the Lord men depart from evil.

Proverbs 16:6

Stand therefore, having your loins girt about with truth.

Ephesians 6:14

Howbeit when he, the Spirit of truth, is come, he will guide you into all truth: for he shall not speak of himself; but whatsoever he shall hear, that shall he speak: and he will shew you things to come.

John 16:13

These things write I unto thee, hoping to come unto thee shortly: But if I tarry long, that thou mayest know how thou oughtest to behave thyself in the house of God, which is the church of the living God, the pillar and ground of the truth.

I Timothy 3:14,15

Additional Scripture References

Deut. 32:4; Josh. 24:14; I Sam. 12:24; Ps. 25:10; 57:10; 117:1,2; John 1:14-17; 18:37; Col. 1:1-6; II Thes. 2:1-12; I Tim. 2:1-6; II Tim. 2:24-26; 3:1-7; Heb. 10:26,27; James 1:17,18; I Jn. 4:6; 5:6; II Jn. 1-4

Unbelief

Take heed, brethren, lest there be in any of you an evil heart of unbelief, in departing from the living God.

Hebrews 3:12

For the preaching of the cross is to them that perish foolishness; but unto us which are saved it is the power of God.

I Corinthians 1:18

O Jerusalem, Jerusalem, which killest the prophets, and stonest them that are sent unto thee; how often would I have gathered thy children together, as a hen doth gather her brood under her wings, and ye would not!

Luke 13:34

Be ye not unequally yoked together with unbelievers: for what fellowship hath righteousness with unrighteousness? and what communion hath light with darkness?

II Corinthians 6:14

I said therefore unto you, that ye shall die in your sins: for if ye believe not that I am he, ye shall die in your sins.

John 8:24

He that believeth on the Son of God hath the witness in himself: he that believeth not God hath made him a liar; because he believeth not the record that God gave of his Son.

I John 5:10

But the fearful, and unbelieving, and the abominable, and murderers, and whoremongers, and sorcerers, and idolaters, and all liars, shall have their part in the lake which burneth with fire and brimstone: which is the second death.

Revelation 21:8

See that ye refuse not him that speaketh. For if they escaped not who refused him that spake on earth, much more shall not we escape, if we turn away from him that speaketh from heaven.

Hebrews 12:25

But without faith it is impossible to please him: for he that cometh to God must believe that he is, and that he is a rewarder of them that diligently seek him.

Hebrews 11:6

Additional Scripture References

Ps. 78:19-33; Jer. 5:10-14; Matt. 10:14,15; 13:13; 13:57,58; John 1:10,11; 5:37,38; 5:46,47; 12:37-41; 12:44-50; Rom. 3:1-4; 14:23; II Thes. 2:1-12; Heb. 3:15-19; 4:1-11; I Pet. 2:7,8

Wealth - Riches

But thou shalt remember the Lord thy God: for it is he that giveth thee power to get wealth, that he may establish his covenant which he sware unto thy fathers, as it is this day.

Deuteronomy 8:18

The Lord maketh poor, and maketh rich: he bringeth low, and lifteth up.

I Samuel 2:7

He becometh poor that dealeth with a slack hand: but the hand of the diligent maketh rich.

Proverbs 10:4

And the disciples were astonished at his words. But Jesus answereth again, and saith unto them, Children, how hard is it for them that trust in riches to enter into the kingdom of God! It is easier for a camel to go through the eye of a needle, than for a rich man to enter into the kingdom of God.

Mark 10:24,25

Praise ye the Lord. Blessed is the man that feareth the Lord, that delighteth greatly in his commandments. His seed shall be mighty upon earth: the generation of the upright shall be blessed. Wealth and riches shall be in his house: and his righteousness endureth for ever.

Psalm 112: 1-3

Labour not to be rich: cease from thine own wisdom. Wilt thou set thine eyes upon that which is not? for riches certainly make themselves wings; they fly away as an eagle toward heaven.

Proverbs 23:4,5

As the partridge sitteth on eggs, and hatcheth them not; so he that getteth riches, and not by right, shall leave them in the midst of his days, and at his end shall be a fool.

Jeremiah 17:11

Better is the poor that walketh in his uprightness, than he that is perverse in his ways, though he be rich.

Proverbs 28:6

Additional Scripture References

Gen. 24:34,35; Ps. 49:1-20; 62:10; Prov. 11:4; 11:28; 15:6; 18:11; 19:4; 21:17; 22:1-4; 28:19-22; 30:8,9; Ecc. 5:8-20; Jer. 9:22-24; Mal. 3:10; Matt. 6:19-21; Mark 4:1-20; Luke 6:22-26; 12:6-21; I Tim. 6:5-11; 6:17-19; James 1:9-11; 5:1-6; I Jn. 3:17; Rev. 3:14-18

Wisdom

The fear of the Lord is the beginning of wisdom: a good understanding have all they that do his commandments: his praise endureth for ever.

Psalm 111:10

If any of you lack wisdom, let him ask of God, that giveth to all men liberally, and upbraideth not; and it shall be given him.

James 1:5

Happy is the man that findeth wisdom, and the man that getteth understanding. For the merchandise of it is better than the merchandise of silver, and the gain thereof than fine gold.

Proverbs 3:13,14

Then said Jesus to those Jews which believed on him, If ye continue in my word, then are ye my disciples indeed; And ye shall know the truth, and the truth shall make you free.

John 8:31,32

But the wisdom that is from above is first pure, then peaceable, gentle, and easy to be intreated, full of mercy and good fruits, without partiality, and without hypocrisy.

James 3:17

How much better is it to get wisdom than gold! and to get understanding rather to be chosen than silver!

Proverbs 16:16

Wisdom strengtheneth the wise more than ten mighty men which are in the city.

Ecclesiastes 7:19

The lips of the righteous feed many: but fools die for want of wisdom.

Proverbs 10:21

For God, who commanded the light to shine out of darkness, hath shined in our hearts, to give the light of the knowledge of the glory of God in the face of Jesus Christ.

II Corinthians 4:6

Wisdom is good with an inheritance: and by it there is profit to them that see the sun. For wisdom is a defence, and money is a defence: but the excellency of knowledge is, that wisdom giveth life to them that have it.

Ecclesiastes 7:11,12

Additional Scripture References

II Chr. 1:6-12; Job 28:12-28; Prov. 2:1-22; 3:13-24; 9:1-6; 19:8; Ecc. 8:1; 9:13-18; John 16:13; I Cor. 1:17-31; 2:9-13; I Tim. 2:1-4; II Pet. 1:2-8

Witnessing

And they overcame him by the blood of the Lamb, and by the word of their testimony; and they loved not their lives unto the death.

Revelation 12:11

Let your light so shine before men, that they may see your good works, and glorify your Father which is in heaven.

Matthew 5:16

And let us not be weary in well doing: for in due season we shall reap, if we faint not.

Galatians 6:9

Sing unto the Lord, bless his name; shew forth his salvation from day to day. Declare his glory among the heathen, his wonders among all people.

Psalm 96:2,3

Brethren, if any of you do err from the truth, and one convert him; Let him know, that he which converteth the sinner from the error of his way shall save a soul from death, and shall hide a multitude of sins.

James 5:19,20

And they that be wise shall shine as the brightness of the firmament; and they that turn many to righteousness as the stars for ever and ever.

Daniel 12:3

Go ye therefore, and teach all nations, baptizing them in the name of the Father, and of the Son, and of the Holy Ghost: Teaching them to observe all things whatsoever I have commanded you: and, lo, I am with you alway, even unto the end of the world. Amen.

Matthew 28:19,20

Then saith he unto his disciples, The harvest truly is plenteous, but the labourers are few; Pray ye therefore the Lord of the harvest, that he will send forth labourers into his harvest.

Matthew 9:37,38

But ye shall receive power, after that the Holy Ghost is come upon you: and ye shall be witnesses unto me both in Jerusalem, and in all Judaea, and in Samaria, and unto the uttermost part of the earth.

Acts 1:8

The fruit of the righteous is a tree of life; and he that winneth souls is wise.

Proverbs 11:30

Additional Scripture References

Mark 8:35; Luke 2:17; 2:38; John 4:35,36; 15:27; Acts 5:32; 26:15-20

Worldliness

Love not the world, neither the things that are in the world. If any man love the world, the love of the Father is not in him. For all that is in the world, the lust of the flesh, and the lust of the eyes, and the pride of life, is not of the Father, but is of the world.

I John 2:15,16

For the grace of God that bringeth salvation hath appeared to all men, Teaching us that, denying ungodliness and worldly lusts, we should live soberly, righteously, and godly, in this present world.

Titus 2:11,12

But if our gospel be hid, it is hid to them that are lost: In whom the god of this world hath blinded the minds of them which believe not, lest the light of the glorious gospel of Christ, who is the image of God, should shine unto them.

II Corinthians 4:3,4

If the world hate you, ye know that it hated me before it hated you. If ye were of the world, the world would love his own: but because ye are not of the world, but I have chosen you out of the world, therefore the world hateth you.

John 15:18,19

(For many walk, of whom I have told you often, and now tell you even weeping, that they are the enemies of the cross of Christ: Whose end is destruction, whose God is their belly, and whose glory is in their shame, who mind earthly things.)

Philippians 3:18,19

And be not conformed to this world: but be ye transformed by the renewing of your mind, that ye may prove what is that good, and acceptable, and perfect, will of God.

Romans 12:2

If ye then be risen with Christ, seek those things which are above, where Christ sitteth on the right hand of God. Set your affection on things above, not on things on the earth.

Colossians 3:1,2

Additional Scripture References

Prov. 21:17; 23:20,21; Is. 5:11,12; 47:6-15; Matt. 6:19,20; 13:22; John 1:10; 3:17; 8:23; 12:25; 14:16,17; 16:33; 17:14-16; 18:36; I Cor. 2:6; 2:12; 3:18,19; Gal. 6:8; Eph. 6:12; II Tim. 2:3,4; James 1:27; 4:4; I Jn. 4:4-7; 5:19

Worshipping God

All the earth shall worship thee, and shall sing unto thee; they shall sing to thy name. Selah.

Psalm 66:4

But the hour cometh, and now is, when the true worshippers shall worship the Father in spirit and in truth: for the Father seeketh such to worship him. God is a Spirit: and they that worship him must worship him in spirit and in truth.

John 4:23,24

And it shall come to pass, that from one new moon to another, and from one sabbath to another, shall all flesh come to worship before me, saith the Lord.

Isaiah 66:23

And thou shalt rejoice before the Lord thy God, thou, and thy son, and thy daughter, and thy manservant, and thy maidservant, and the Levite that is within thy gates, and the stranger, and the fatherless, and the widow, that are among you, in the place which the Lord thy God hath chosen to place his name there.

Deuteronomy 16:11

Exalt ye the Lord our God, and worship at his footstool; for he is holy ... Exalt the Lord our God, and worship at his holy hill; for the Lord our God is holy.

Psalm 99:5,9

Enter into his gates with thanksgiving, and into his courts with praise: be thankful unto him, and bless his name.

Psalm 100:4

For thou shalt worship no other god: for the Lord, whose name is Jealous, is a jealous God.

Exodus 34:14

Give unto the Lord the glory due unto his name: bring an offering, and come before him: worship the Lord in the beauty of holiness.

I Chronicles 16:29

I will praise thee with my whole heart: before the gods will I sing praise unto thee. I will worship toward thy holy temple, and praise thy name for thy lovingkindness and for thy truth: for thou hast magnified thy word above all thy name.

Psalm 138:1,2

Additional Scripture References

Ex. 29:42,43; Lev. 19:30; Deut. 31:11-13; Ps. 5:7; 24:3,4; 27:4; 35:18; 48:9; 55:14; 65:4; 103:1-5; 116:17-19; 122:1; Ecc. 5:1; Is. 56:7; Hab. 2:20; Matt. 4:10; 18:20; Luke 24:51-53; Acts 5:42; 12:12; I Tim. 2:8; Heb. 10:24,25

Adultery

Ex. 20:14; Lev. 20:10; Deut. 5:18;
Job 24:15-20; Prov. 5:15-23; 6:20-35; 30:20;
Is. 57:3-21; Jer. 5:7-9; 7:8-34; 23:14-16;
Ezek. 23:43-49; Mal. 3:5; Matt. 5:27-32;
15:16-20; Rom. 13:8,9; I Cor. 6:9,10;
Gal. 5:19-21; Heb. 13:4; James 4:4

Anger

Ps. 37:8; Prov. 12:16; 14:29; 15:1; 15:18;
16:32; 19:11; 19:19; 21:24; 22:24; 25:28; 27:3,4;
29:8; 29:22; 30:33; Ecc. 7:9; Matt. 5:22-24;
Rom. 12:19; Gal. 5:19-21; Eph. 4:31,32;
Col. 3:1-14; I Tim. 2:8; James 1:19,20

Backsliding

Deut. 4:25,26; I Kin. 11:9; Ps. 78:56-61; 85:8;
101:3; 125:5; Prov. 14:14; 28:9,10; 28:14;
Is. 59:1,2; Jer. 2:19; 3:11-14; 3:20-22; 8:5;
15:6; Mark 9:50; Luke 9:62; I Cor. 10:12;
II Cor. 11:3; Gal. 5:1; Col. 1:21-23; 2:8;
Heb. 6:4-6; II Pet. 1:4-11; 2:20-22; II Jn. 8,9;
Rev. 2:4

Baptism

Matt. 3:5,6; 3:11; 3:13-17; 28:19,20; Mark 1:4;
1:8; 16:16; Luke 3:1-22; 7:29; John 1:29-34;
3:22,23; Acts 1:1-5; 2:38,41; 8:12,13;
8:26-38; 9:1-18; 10:44-48; 16:14,15;
16:22-33; 18:8; 19:1-5; Rom. 6:3-11;
I Cor. 12:1-13; Eph. 4:4-6; Col. 2:9-12;
Titus 3:5

Bitterness

Prov. 14:10; Rom. 3:10-18; Eph. 4:31,32;
Heb. 12:5,6; 12:14,15; James 3:13-16

The Bride of Christ

II Cor. 11:2; Eph. 5:25-32; Col. 1:21,22;
Rev. 19:6-9; Rev. 21:9; Rev. 22:17

Demons

I Sam. 16:14-23; Dan. 10:10-14; Matt. 4:24;
8:28-32; 9:32,33; 17:15-21; 25:41;
Mark 1:23-26; 9:25; Luke 13:11,16; Acts 5:16;
Eph. 6:11,12; I Tim. 4:1; James 2:19;
II Pet. 2:4; Jude 6; Rev. 9:1-11; 16:13,14

Divorce

Mal. 2:14-16; Matt. 5:31,32; 19:3-9;
Mark 10:2-12; Luke 16:18; I Cor. 7:10-17

Drinking-Drunkenness

Lev. 10:8-10; Num. 6:1-4; Deut. 21:17-21;
29:19,20; Prov. 20:1; 21:17; 23:20,21;
23:29-35; 31:4,5; Is. 5:11,12; 5:22; 28:1; 28:7,8;
Ezek. 44:21; Hos. 4:11; Nah. 1:10; Hab. 2:15;
Luke 1:15; 21:34; Rom. 13:13; I Cor. 5:9-11;
6:9,10; 11:20-22; Gal. 5:19-21; Eph. 5:17-21;
I Thes. 5:5-8; I Tim. 3:1-9; Titus 2:11,12;
I Pet. 4:1-7; 5:8

Family

Gen. 2:23,24; 18:19; Ex. 20:12; Lev. 19:3;
Deut. 4:9; 5:16; 6:6,7; 11:18,19; Josh. 24:15;
Est. 1:20,22; Ps. 78:1-7; 127:3-5; Prov. 12:4;
14:1; 15:17; 18:22; 19:13,14; 21:9,19; 25:24;
30:21-23; 31:10-31; Matt. 19:13,14; Luke 17:2;
I Cor. 11:3-12; Eph. 5:22-33; 6:1-4;
Col. 3:18-21; I Tim. 5:8; I Pet. 3:1,2

Fasting

Jud. 20:26; I Sam. 31:13; II Sam. 12:16,17;
II Chr. 20:3; Ezra 8:21-23; Neh. 1:4; Est. 4:15,16;
Ps. 35:13; 69:10; 109:21-24; Is. 58:1-11;
Jer. 36:6; Dan. 6:18; 9:3; Joel 1:1-15; 2:12-27;
Jonah 3:5; Matt. 4:1,2; 6:16-18; 9:14-16;
17:14-21; Luke 2:36-38; Acts 13:1-3; 14:23

Fornication

Matt. 15:19,20; Mark 7:20-23; Acts 15:28,29;
Rom. 1:18-32; I Cor. 5:1-13; 6:9-20; 7:2;
10:1-12; II Cor. 12:20,21; Gal. 5:19-21;
Eph. 5:1-7; Col. 3:5-10; I Thes. 4:3; Jude 7,8;
Rev. 2:14; 2:20

Homosexuality

Gen. 19:1-13; Lev. 18:22-30; 20:13;
Jud. 19:22-30; Rom. 1:18-32; I Cor. 6:9;
I Tim. 1:8-10

Miracles

*Ex. 7:10-12; Ps. 78:12-16; 105:5; Is. 29:14;
Jer. 32:17-21; Matt. 7:22,23; 9:28,29; 12:28;
12:38; 17:19,20; 21:21,22; 24:24; Mark 3:14,15;
9:23; 16:17-20; John 3:2; 4:48; 14:12;
Acts 3:1-16; 4:29,30; 6:8; 14:3; 14:8-10; 15:12;
19:11; Rom. 15:18,19; I Cor. 12:7-10;
12:28-30; II Cor. 12:12; II Thes. 2:3,4; 2:8-10;
Rev. 13:1-18; 16:13,14; 19:20*

Offerings

*Gen. 4:1-7; 22:2; Ex. 25:2; 29:15-18;
29:24-28; 29:42; Lev. 1:1-8; 22:21-25;
Num. 6:10-17; 7:1-88; 10:10; Ps. 51:16-19;
96:8; Is. 1:10-18; 66:20; Jer. 14:10-12;
Mal. 1:1-14; 3:8-12; Acts 21:26; Eph. 5:2;
Heb. 10:1-18*

Profanity

*Ex. 20:7; Lev. 19:12; Deut. 5:11;
Ps. 139:20-22; Ecc. 10:12,13; Jer. 23:10-12;
Matt. 5:33-37; Col. 4:6; I Tim. 4:7; 6:20,21;
II Tim. 2:15,16; James 5:12*

Sacrifices

Gen. 31:54; 46:1; Ps. 4:5; 40:5,6; 51:16,17; 107:22; 116:17; Prov. 15:8; 21:3; 21:27; Ecc. 5:1; Jer. 33:10,11; Hos. 6:6; Rom. 12:1; Eph. 5:1,2; Phil. 3:7,8; Heb. 10:18-22; 13:15,16; I Pet. 2:5

Selfishness

Gen. 4:9; Num. 32:6; Ps. 38:11; Prov. 11:25,26; 18:17; 28:27; Is. 5:8; Zech. 7:4-6; Matt. 19:21; Luke 12:32-36; Rom. 15:1-3; I Cor. 10:24; II Cor. 5:15; Gal. 6:2; Phil. 2:3-8; 2:20,21; I Thes. 5:14,15; II Tim. 3:1-5; James 2:15,16; 3:17

Self Righteousness

Deut. 9:4-6; Prov. 12:15; 14:12; 16:2; 20:6; 25:14; 25:27; 26:12; 27:2; 28:26; 30:12,13; Is. 5:21; 64:6; 65:2-5; Jer. 2:22-25; Hos. 12:8; Zeph. 3:11; Matt. 7:22,23; Luke 16:15; 18:9-14; Rom. 2:17-24; 3:27; 10:3; 12:3; II Cor. 10:17,18; Gal. 6:3

Self Will

*II Kin. 17:14; II Chr. 30:8; Ps. 32:9; 75:5-7;
Prov. 1:22-27; Is. 42:24; Jer. 7:23,24;
Zech. 7:11-14; Acts 7:51; Titus 1:7;
Heb. 3:7-12; II Pet. 2:9,10*

Waiting on the Lord

*Ps. 25:1-5; 27:14; 33:20; 37:7-9; 40:1; 59:9;
62:1-8; 104:24-28; 123:2; 130:5,6; 145:15,16;
Prov. 20:22; Is. 30:18; 40:31; 64:4; Jer. 14:22;
Lam. 3:25,26; Hos. 12:6; Mic. 7:7; Hab. 2:2,3;
Acts 1:4; Gal. 5:5; II Pet. 3:8*

Where to Find it in the Bible....

Prophecies Concerning Jesus

Seed of Woman	Gen.	3:15
Seed of Abraham	Gen.	12:3
		18:18
Of Tribe of Judah	Gen.	49:10
Seed of Jacob	Num.	24:17,19
Seed of David	Ps.	132:11
	Is.	11:10
	Jer.	23:5
		33:15
A Prophet	Deut.	18:15,19
Son of God	Ps.	2:7
	Prov.	30:4
To Be Raised from the Dead	Ps.	16:10
Crucifixion	Ps.	69:21
Betrayal	Ps.	41:9
Ascension	Ps.	68:18
Tribute from Kings	Ps.	72:10,11
A Priest Like Melchizedek	Ps.	110:4
At the Right Hand of God	Ps.	110:1
Stone Rejected	Ps.	118:22,23
(Head Cornerstone)	Is.	8:14,15
		28:16
Born of a Virgin	Is.	7:14
Galilee Ministry	Is.	9:1-8
To Be Meek and Mild	Is.	42:2,3
		53:7
Minister to the Gentiles	Is.	42:1
		49:1-8
To Be Smitten	Is.	50:6
Suffering	Is.	52:13-53:12

New Covenant	Is.	55:3,4
	Jer.	31:31-33
Right Arm of God	Is.	53:1
		59:16
Intercessor	Is.	59:16
Mission	Is.	61:1-11
To Perform Miracles	Is.	35:5,6
Called "The Lord"	Jer.	23:5,6
Time of His Coming	Dan.	9:24-26
Place of Birth	Mic.	5:2
Will Enter the Temple	Mal.	3:1
Enter Jerusalem on a Donkey	Zech.	9:9
To Be Pierced	Ps.	22:16
	Zech.	12:10
Forsaken By Disciples	Zech.	13:7
Opposed By Nations	Ps.	2:2
Victory Over Death	Is.	25:8
Glorious In Apparel	Is.	63:1
As King	Ps.	2:6-9
Submission of Nations	Is.	2:4
	Mic.	4:1-4
Gentiles To Seek	Is.	11:10

The Life of Jesus

Birth of Jesus	Matt.	1:18-2:11
	Luke	1:26-56
		2:1-20
Escape from Bethlehem	Matt.	2:12-23
Jesus As A Boy	Luke	2:40-52
Baptism of Jesus	Matt.	3:1-17
	Mark	1:9-11
	Luke	3:1-22
Temptation of Jesus	Matt.	4:1-11
	Mark	1:12,13
	Luke	4:1-13
Sermon on the Mount	Matt.	5:1-7:29
	Luke	6:20-49
Walking on Water	Matt.	14:22-33
	Mark	6:45-52
	John	6:16-21
Transfiguration	Matt.	17:1-13
	Mark	9:2-8
Triumphal Entry Into Jerusalem	Matt.	21:1-11
	Mark	11:1-11
	Luke	19:29-44
	John	12:12-19
The Last Supper	Matt.	26:17-30
	Mark	14:12-25
	Luke	22:7-38
Gethsemane	Matt.	26:36-46
	Mark	14:32-42
	Luke	22:39-46
Prayer of Intercession	John	17:1-26

Betrayal of Jesus	Matt.	26:47-49
	Mark	14:43-45
	Luke	22:47,48
Arrest of Jesus	Matt.	26:49-56
	Mark	14:46-50
	Luke	22:54-65
	John	18:1-11
Trial of Jesus	Matt.	26:57-27:26
	Mark	14:53-15:20
	Luke	22:66-23:25
	John	18:12-19:16
Crucifixion and Death of Jesus	Matt.	27:27-66
	Mark	15:21-47
	Luke	23:26-56
	John	19:17-42
Resurrection	Matt.	28:1-10
	Mark	16:1-8
	Luke	24:1-12
	John	20:1-10
Post-Resurrection Appearances	Matt.	28:16-20
	Mark	16:9-18
	Luke	24:13-49
	John	20:11-21:25
	Acts	1:1-8
Jesus' Ascension	Mark	16:19,20
	Luke	24:50-53
	Acts	1:9-11

Miracles of Jesus

Water Into Wine	John	2:1-11
Healing Nobleman's Son	John	4:46-54
Healing Lame Man	John	5:1-9
Miraculous Catch of Fish	Luke	5:1-11
Delivering Demoniac	Mark	1:23-28
	Luke	4:31-36
Peter's Mother-in-law	Matt.	8:14,15
	Mark	1:29-31
	Luke	4:38,39
Cleansing the Leper	Matt.	8:2-4
	Mark	1:40-45
	Luke	5:12-16
Healing a Paralytic	Matt.	9:2-8
	Mark	2:3-12
	Luke	5:18-26
Man with Withered Hand	Matt.	12:9-13
	Mark	3:1-5
	Luke	6:6-10
Centurion's Servant	Matt.	8:5-13
	Luke	7:1-10
Raising Widow's Son	Luke	7:11-15
Blind and Dumb Demoniac	Matt.	12:22
	Luke	11:14
Stilling the Storm	Matt.	8:18,23-27
	Mark	4:35-41
	Luke	8:22-25
Delivering Demoniacs	Matt.	8:28-34
	Mark	5:1-20
	Luke	8:26-39

Man with Dropsy	Luke	14:1-6
Raising Lazarus	John	11:17-44
Cleansing Ten Lepers	Luke	17:11-19
Blind Bartimaeus	Matt.	20:29-34
	Mark	10:46-52
	Luke	18:35-43
Cursing the Fig Tree	Matt.	21:18,19
	Mark	11:12-14
Restoring Malchus' Ear	Luke	22:49-51
	John	18:10
Second Catch of Fish	John	21:1-11

Parables of Jesus

The Sower	Matt.	13:3-8
	Mark	4:3-8
	Luke	8:5-8
The Tares	Matt.	13:24-30
Mustard Seed	Matt.	13:31,32
	Mark	4:31,32
	Luke	13:19
The Leaven	Matt.	13:33
	Luke	13:21
The Hid Treasure	Matt.	13:44
The Pearl of Great Price	Matt.	13:45,46
The Drag Net	Matt.	13:47-50
The Unmerciful Servant	Matt.	18:23-35
The Vineyard Laborers	Matt.	20:1-6
The Two Sons	Matt.	21:28-32
The Wicked Husbandman	Matt.	21:33-46
	Mark	12:1-12
	Luke	20:9-19

Marriage of the King's Son	Matt.	22:1-14
The Ten Virgins	Matt.	25:1-13
The Talents	Matt.	25:14-30
The Seed Growing	Mark	4:26-29
The Two Debtors	Luke	7:41-43
The Good Samaritan	Luke	10:25-37
The Friend at Midnight	Luke	11:5-8
The Rich Fool	Luke	12:16-21
The Barren Fig Tree	Luke	13:6-9
The Great Supper	Luke	14:16-24
The Lost Sheep	Matt.	18:12-14
	Luke	15:4-7
The Lost Money	Luke	15:8-10
The Prodigal Son	Luke	15:11-32
The Unjust Steward	Luke	16:1-9
The Rich Man and Lazarus	Luke	16:19-31
The Unprofitable Servants	Luke	17:7-10
The Unjust Judge	Luke	18:1-8
The Pharisee and the Publican	Luke	18:10-14
The Pounds	Luke	19:12-27

Where to Find It

- NOTES -

- NOTES -

- NOTES -

- NOTES -

- NOTES -

- NOTES -

- NOTES -

- NOTES -

- NOTES -

- NOTES -

- NOTES -

- NOTES -